THE FLY TIER'S MANUAL

Mike Dawes is an experienced fly fisherman who has fished extensively all over the world. He is the proprietor of Graham Trout Flies of Herefordshire, one of the largest distributors of fishing flies in Great Britain, selling over one million flies each year. A keen sporting photographer, he has contributed to several books, magazines and periodicals. All the flies in the book were photographed by him.

THE
FLY TIER'S
MANUAL

MIKE DAWES

FLY PATTERN DRAWINGS BY TAFF PRICE

CollinsWillow

An Imprint of HarperCollins*Publishers*

CollinsWillow
an imprint of HarperCollins*Publishers*
London

First published 1985
Reprinted 1992
First published in paperback 1995
Reprinted 1997 1998 2001

The Fly Tier's Manual has been designed and
produced by Johnston & Streiffert Editions,
Södermalmsgatan 35, S-431 69 Mölndal,
Sweden

World copyright © 1985 Johnston & Streiffert
Editions

Photography: Mike Dawes
Artwork: Taff Price

A CIP catalogue record for this book is available from the British Library

ISBN: 0 00 218728 0

Manufactured in Italy

Author's Acknowledgments

I dedicate this book to my wife, Ali, whose patience, help, and
encouragement—even when I had taken over half the house as a
photographic studio—made it all possible.

My sincere thanks go to Taff Price for the superb line
drawings which contribute so much to the book. My gratitude
also goes to Taff for his expert knowledge, which he was always
happy to share with me and thus with the readers of this book.
His familiarity with patterns from all over the world has been of
enormous assistance, as has his mastery of entomology and of
some very tricky tying problems that arose during the com-
pilation of the patterns.

I must also take this opportunity of thanking Bev Harper-
Smith for many of the beautifully tied flies that appear in this
book. They are an example, and a challenge, to the reader.

Throughout the years, I have written to, and received many
letters from, flytying enthusiasts from all over the world—
thoughtful, informative, and often helpfully critical letters
from people who care passionately about their hobby and sport.
I look forward to hearing from any reader who might have
something to add to any of the patterns given here. Active
feedback from readers will make the task of providing a revised
edition, should there be a demand for one, easier.

Mike Dawes
Graham Trout Flies
Herefordshire

Contents

I

Equipment, Materials, and Basic Methods

I

Equipment, Materials, and Basic Methods

To the uninitiated, it might appear a trifle absurd that a fisherman should take thread, scraps of feathers, and bits of different-coloured fur and other materials, and tie them on a hook with the intention of fooling a fish into believing that this is its favourite food. Be that as it may, this is what many fishermen have been doing for centuries, and more and more in our lifetime. Flytying, or fly dressing, is considered by many people to be something of an art. The word "art" might put some people off, while others may want to reach for their gun when they hear it, but call it an art or not, there is nothing more satisfying than catching a fish on a fly that you yourself have tied. And the more flies you tie, the more you learn about the natural fly, and the better you are able to pick an artificial fly to match the flies that are active on the river or lake that you are fishing.

To be able to tie a fly, you do not have to have a surgeon's delicate touch or dexterity. In fact, one of the best flytiers I know has enormous hands, yet he ties the most exquisite flies right down to a size 22. The great G.E.M. Skues had fingers that have been described as short, thick carrots, yet he could tie the smallest of flies up until the age of ninety. No mean feat, when you consider that he was blind in one eye...

What the beginner needs to remember is that he should always tie, say, six of every pattern he tries. By the time he gets to the sixth, he will have ironed out the faults in his technique and will have found the right way to handle the materials. Practice makes as near perfect as you will ever come! And in the long winter evenings, what better pastime is there than to see to it that your fly box is filled and ready for all eventualities when the season opens.

In the beginning, you should take a course in flytying or get a friend to introduce you to the tricks of the trade. This will make your first steps in flytying easier, and the advice of someone experienced will help you to avoid getting into bad habits which will be difficult to get rid of later on. Learning to tie flies is a bit like learning to play golf: a little coaching goes a long way.

Equipment

The essential tools for flytying are neither many nor costly. As the tools are not expensive, you should buy the best that money can buy. Good-quality tools, being more reliable, will give you confidence and will, if you treat them with care, last a lifetime. If in doubt about what to buy, go to a well-stocked tackle shop where the staff is known to be knowledgeable and friendly, and ask them to advise you. Having friends in a tackle shop is a worthwhile investment: you can get a lot of good advice and help from them. And as it is becoming more and more difficult to get hold of the rarer flytying materials, it is always good to have a friend in the supply chain who will keep a rarity tucked away for you until you come by.

The vice

A good vice will hold the hook firmly in position while allowing your fingers the room to work freely. The vice is your most essential piece of equipment, so be prepared to pay as much as you can afford, and buy a reputable make. If possible, try out the vice before you buy it (ask a friend who has one to let you work on it, or go into your friendly tackle shop when they are not busy). Remember that there are far more bad-quality than good-quality vices on the market, so it is worth your while to be pernickety about it.

Scissors

These are your next most important tools. One pair should be for heavy duty, such as cutting quills and coarse materials like tinsel. Good-quality medium-sized manicure or pedicure scissors will do.

The other pair of scissors should be somewhat smaller and have slightly curved blades of the highest-quality steel. It should be used only for trimming hackles closely and for working with fine materials. Sharp-pointed surgical scissors are the best bet here.

The dubbing needle

This is simply a sewing needle with a handle at the eye end. It is an extremely all-round tool, being useful for many of the small jobs that you will have to do: applying varnish or cement to a head, separating fibres on a feather quill, "fuzzing up" the fur on a fly body, spreading dubbing material on the thread, and so on.

You can buy a dubbing needle, but it is simple to make your own. Take a suitable piece of dowel (wood is best), drill a small hole in one end and fill it with epoxy cement, and push the eye end of a sewing needle into the hole. When the cement has hardened, the needle is ready to be used.

Hackle pliers

This is simply a spring holder with which you hold the hackle by its tip when you are winding it around the body of the fly. More experienced flytiers often prefer to use their fingers, as they want to have the "feel" of the tension as they wind on the hackle. If they are winding on a mixture of materials, this "feel" is important because each material has to be kept under a different tension, and the jaws of the hackle pliers are insensitive to this.

The jaws of the hackle pliers should close together over as much of their length as possible, and the edges of the jaws should not be sharp. In fact, many pliers have rubber-covered edges to protect the sensitive hackles.

The bobbin holder

The tying thread has to be kept taut throughout the operation. If you let go of the thread while preparing some material, it can unwind. This can be avoided by tying a half-hitch every time you let go of the thread, but this is time-consuming and can produce a body that is too bulky. The bobbin holder holds the tying-thread spool so that the thread is under tension all the time, yet can be pulled from the spool as it is required.

The whip-finisher

A neat whip-finished head is a must if your fly is to be durable and not unravel after a few casts. A whip-finishing tool can help you do this in the beginning (instructions on how to use one are always sold with the tool), but the method on page 13 is easy to learn.

Materials

All the materials mentioned in the patterns in this book are available in any well-stocked tackle shop. One of the pitfalls for the beginner is to buy too much material and too many different types. Keeping a neat and orderly desk, drawer, or box of materials will save you much irritation. So start off by buying just what you need for the first series of flies that you are going to tie. Label each piece of material clearly and use some kind of system (alphabetical is the simplest) so that you can find them at will.

A special vocabulary has been developed by flytiers over the centuries to describe the different tones and hues of the feathers and other material that they work with: dun, honey, honey dun, pale blue dun, and so on. The best way to familiarize yourself with these different shades is to build up a collection of feathers that you buy from your tackle shop. If you happen to be a hunter, then you have a ready-made supply when you shoot pheasant, partridge, grouse, mallard, or teal, but it is important that you can identify the actual hues, so that you use the right feather for the right fly.

Dry-fly Wing Styles

1

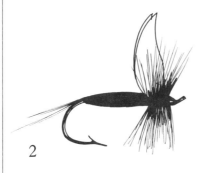

2

3

1. Hackled dry (no wing)

2. Upright split wing

3. Sedge wing

4

5

6

4. Upright hackle point

5. Spent hackle point

6. Fan wing

7

8

9

7. Upright hair wing

8. Hair wing sedge

9. Spent fibre wing (hair or feather fibres)

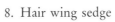

Dry Fly Winging (upright split wing)

1.

Two slips of wing quill are placed on top of the hook and held there by the thumb and first finger of the left hand. Three turns of tying thread secure them.

2.

With the same two fingers, raise the feather slips to the vertical position and take three turns of tying thread on the other side. Some maintain that the wings should now be divided by means of a figure-of-eight turn of thread between each wing slip. I have found that this is not necessary; by carefully easing the slips apart with a dubbing needle, the natural outcurve of most wing slips keeps them separated.

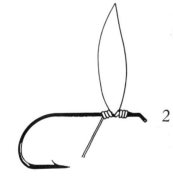

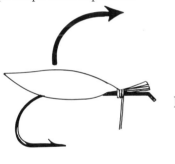

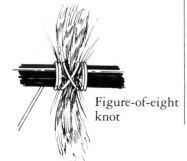

Figure-of-eight knot

Types of Hackle

1. The *dry-fly hackle* is a cock hackle wound in a full circle around the hook, just behind the eye. It supports the fly on the surface and simulates the wings and legs of the insect.

2. The *wet-fly hackle* is a soft hen or game-bird hackle wound around the hook, collar-style. The soft hackle moves and pulsates in the water, giving life to the fly.

3. The *false, or beard, hackle* is tied beneath the hook to simulate the legs of the insect.

4. The *palmered hackle* is one of the oldest hackle designs. The hackle is tied along the shank. It gives extra support to dry flies and extra "movement" to wet.

5. The *skater hackle* is tied with an extra-long hackle that keeps the hook out of the water. The fly can move very naturally with the water or when pulled with the rod.

1

2

3

4

5

Starting the Fly

The first step in tying any fly is to lay down a whipping of tying thread along the hook shank. Place the hook in the vice. Check the hook's temper by flicking the hook with your fingers. If it is under-tempered, it will be soft and have a tendency to bend in the vice. If over-tempered, it will be brittle and more often than not will break in the vice. A correctly tempered hook will ring true with a distinct "ping" when flicked with the finger.

1.

Take the bobbin holder and pull off some thread with the left hand. Offer the thread to the hook.

2, 3.

Still holding the loose end of tying thread in the thumb and finger in the left hand, revolve the bobbin holder around the hook shank.

4.

Continue this winding around the hook shank, trapping in the loose end as you go along. When you have laid a satisfactory amount of whipping along the shank, cut off the loose end of thread (if any).

You now have a bed of tying thread on which to apply the fur and feather. The bed of thread makes it easier to tie on wings, tails, and so on, securely.

Normally, you use a thread that is already waxed when you buy it. It is only rarely that the pattern requires a specially waxed thread (but see, for instance, Greenwell's Glory on page 75, which specifically states cobbler's wax, to discolour the yellow thread so that it becomes greenish-yellow).

One essential point to remember when tying the rest of the fly: The ribbing should *always* be wound in the opposite direction to that in which the body material was wound. Not only does this make the body more secure, but also the ribbing will not then sink into the body material and be covered.

The mark of a well-tied fly is its even and regular ribbing.

Dubbing

Some fly dressers mix large quantities of dubbing fur at the same time in a domestic blender. This is an excellent way of thoroughly mixing different types or tones of fur to get just the mixture or colour that you want. The following method shows how to spin dubbing fur onto the tying thread.

If you are trying to copy the colour of a natural, remember that you should compare both in the wet state. That is how they will be in or on the water. Spin some of the dubbing onto a piece of thread, wind it onto a hook, and wet the hook. Now compare the wet body with that of the natural, which you should have in water.

1.

Apply some wax to the tying thread. As mentioned above, this is not necessary if a ready-waxed thread is used. Take a pinch of the fur to be dubbed and offer it to the thread.

2.

This is easy if you support the thread and fur with the forefinger.

3.

Spin the fur and thread into a rope with a squeezing, rolling action. It is vital that the rolling action is in one direction only (*either* clockwise or anticlockwise). More fur can be added if you want a bushy body. (It is better to apply the fur in small portions rather than all in one large mass.)

4.

The finished dubbed thread should look like this.

5.

The fur-laden thread is now wound, around the hook shank, back up towards the eye, to form the body of the fly.

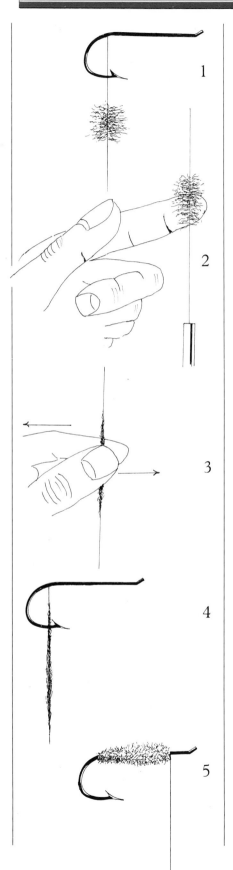

Finishing the Fly

All flies are finished off by what is termed a whip finish, although some flytiers complete their flies by means of a series of half hitches. A neater head is achieved by the whip finish.

1.

Form a loop in the tying thread, holding it open by means of the first two fingers of the right hand.

2.

By rotating the fingers, take the thread over the hook shank, trapping the tying thread.

3.

Repeat the procedure. A normal head on a fly will require three or four turns.

4.

Pull the end of the thread tight and cut flush.

5.

A drop of varnish seals the knot.

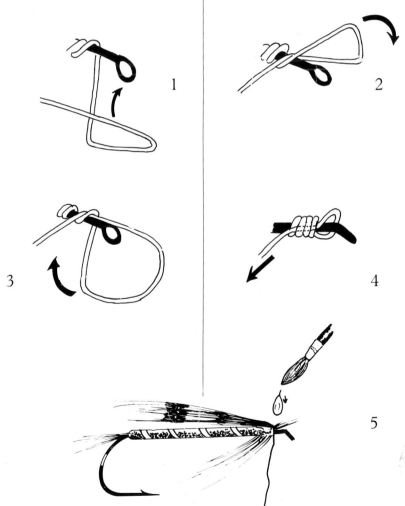

II

Fly Patterns

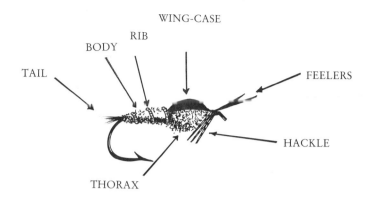

The nymph is considered by the fly-fisherman to be an imitation of any aquatic larva on the river or lake bed, or on its way to the surface to hatch. Some nymphs go directly to the surface, while others do it more slowly, perhaps going from stone to stone before rising. Nymphs form a large part of the trout's diet and that is one of the reasons why nymph fishing has increased enormously in popularity over the years.

There are two basic stages during which the trout feed actively on the natural nymph. First, the active larval stage when the fish feed deep on the stream or lake bed; second, the inert stage, when the mature nymph makes its way to the surface, to split its case and emerge as an adult. The trout then follows it upwards to the surface. As far as the fisherman is concerned, the latter stage is the more important.

In still water, approximately ninety per cent of the trout's diet is made up of nymphs in their larval or inert stages. Also, the nymph is available to the trout for months before that brief moment when it rises to the surface for the last time and casts off its nymphal case to become an adult insect. During their last few days as nymphs, they become restless, rising to the surface and then falling back onto the river or lake bed several times. This activity attracts the trout, who start to gorge themselves. The trouts' activity is easily seen in still waters, as they "head and tail" or "bulge" on the surface.

An interesting development in the tying of nymphs is the fact that a growing number of flytiers are dressing some of their nymphs with lead wire along the shank of the hook before building the actual body. Their reason for this is to get the nymph down quickly to the river or lake bed, where much of the natural nymph's life is spent. This fairly recent modification has met with much success, and most tackle shops now stock such nymphs.

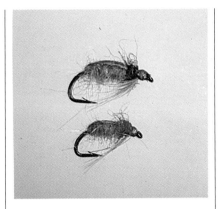

Amber

One of the very earliest imitative patterns designed for lake and reservoir fishing. Originally tied by Dr. Bell of Wrington who fished this nymph very successfully at Blagdon. There is not much doubt that these patterns were tied to imitate the many species of Sedge pupae that are predominantly orangy/brown.

I have illustrated two patterns and the only difference is the colour of the thorax and the hook size.

  Hooks: Down-eyed 10–14
  Thread: Black (larger pattern), yellow (smaller pattern)
  Ribbing: Gold
  Wing-case: Brown feather tied *over* body
  Body: Amber yellow seal's fur
  Thorax: Dark brown (large pattern), hot orange (small pattern)
  Hackle: Honey hen hackle fibres – sloping back under thorax
  Head: Black (large pattern), yellow (small pattern)

1.

As always, start the fly in the usual way by winding the thread down the shank. At the bend of the hook tie in a slip of brown feather. This will be the wing-case. Dub some amber seal's fur onto the tying thread.

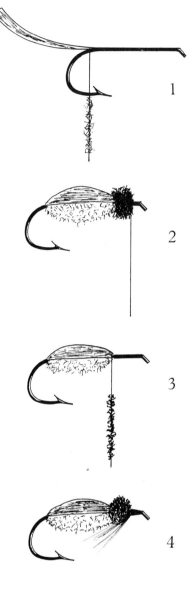

2.

Return the dubbed thread up the shank about two-thirds of the way. Next, take the brown feather over the back and tie off; cut away the surplus. Dub the fur for the thorax, brown for one version, orange for the other, onto the thread.

3.

Form the thorax as shown.

4.

Add a few fibres of light ginger or honey hackle and complete the fly.

American March Brown Nymph

As a natural, the American March Brown (*Stenonema vicarium*) is notable for its stiff tail. When tying the tail, it is a good idea to tie the centre of the three tail fibres first and the other two at an angle of about 45° on each side of the centre fibre. This is tied in the same way as the Catskill Hendrickson (*page 19*).

  Hook: Down-eyed 10 long shank
  Thread: Brown
  Tail: Three elk or cock-pheasant tail fibres
  Body: Amber seal's fur mixed with a small amount of tan fox fur and dubbed on the tying thread
  Thorax: Peacock herl
  Ribbing: Brown embroidery cotton
  Legs: Brown partridge hackle, tied as a false beard
  Wing-case: Cock-pheasant fibres
  Head: Brown

Bloodworm Larva

This is the Taff Price dressing. Trout tend to congregate and feed on the Bloodworm larvae when they emerge from the mud and rise.

> *Hooks*: Down-eyed 12–14
> long shank
> *Thread*: Black
> *Tail*: Red marabou
> *Body*: Red floss with evenly
> spaced bulges along the
> length of the hook
> *Ribbing*: Fluorescent red
> floss
> *Head*: Peacock herl

1.
At the bend of the hook, tie in a bunch of red marabou fibres, about the same length of the hook. Also tie in a length of fluorescent red floss.

2.
Take the tying thread back up the hook shank and tie in a length of red floss.

3.
Take the red floss up and down the hook and wind in such a way as to form little undulations. Rib the valleys of the undulations with the fluorescent red floss. Tie off and, at this point, tie in two strands of bronze peacock herl.

4.
Wind on the head of peacock herl and complete the fly with a small neat head.

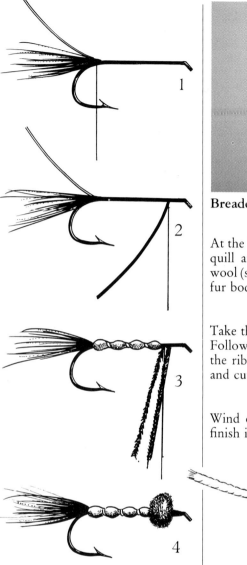

Breadcrust

Originally classified as a wet pattern, this has been found to be more effective when fished as a nymph.

> *Hooks*: Down-eyed 10–14
> *Thread*: Black
> *Body*: Orange wool yarn or
> dubbed synthetic fur
> *Ribbing*: Stripped hackle
> quill
> *Hackle*: Soft grizzle hen
> hackle
> *Head*: Black

Breadcrust

1.
At the bend, tie in a stripped hackle quill and a length of light orange wool (some prefer a dubbed orange-fur body).

2.
Take the thread back up the shank. Follow with the wool and, finally, the ribbing of hackle stalk. Tie off and cut off surplus.

3.
Wind on a grizzle hen hackle and finish in the usual way.

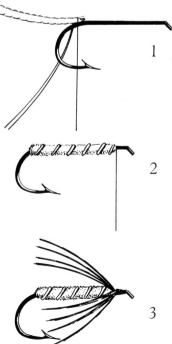

Brown Bomber

A popular pattern from the east coast of America, used a lot on still waters.

> *Hooks*: Down-eyed 10–12 long shank
> *Thread*: Brown
> *Body*: Dubbed muskrat fur with guard hairs removed (take the fur from its back)
> *Ribbing*: Flat gold tinsel
> *Hackle*: Brown partridge
> *Head*: Brown

1.
Take the thread down to the bend of the hook.

2.
At the same place, tie in a length of flat gold tinsel.

3.
Dub the thread with the muskrat fur and wind back down the hook shank to form the body.

4.
Follow with the flat gold tinsel and tie off.

5.
Tie in the brown partridge hackle.

6.
Whip and varnish.

Buzzer

Buzzers, or Chironomids, are the curved black flies usually found over still water in the evenings. They appear rather menacing but are in fact quite harmless. This is one of the simplest patterns.

The pupa stage is by far the most successful pattern and the various colours are legion.

> *Hooks*: Down-eyed 10–14
> *Thread*: Black
> *Body*: Black floss silk
> *Ribbing*: Flat silver tinsel
> *Thorax*: Bronze peacock herl
> *Breathing Filaments*: White cock hackle fibres (or white fluorescent floss silk)
> *Tail Filaments* (optional): White cock hackle fibres (or white floss silk)

1.
Take the tying thread partly around the bend of the hook. If you wish, tie in either a small tuft of white cock hackle fibres, white floss silk, or even fine white wool.

2.
Take the thread halfway up the hook shank and tie in a length of body floss and a length of ribbing tinsel—most prefer flat silver for buzzer flies.

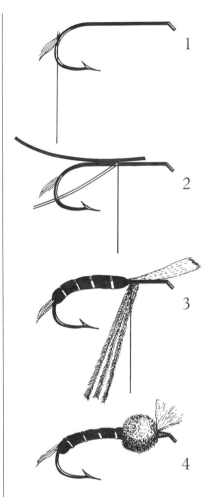

3.
Return the thread right around the bend, trapping in the body floss and ribbing medium. Take the tying thread once more up the hook. Follow with the body floss and subsequently the rib, tie off, and remove surplus materials. At this stage, tie in a tuft of white fluorescent floss (or white feather fibres) and three strands of peacock herl.

4.
Form a rotund thorax with the peacock herl, leaving the white floss or feather fibre extended over the eye of the hook. Finish off the fly as usual.

Body-floss colour alternatives: black, red, orange, green, olive, and brown.

Catskill Hendrickson

This is yet another nymph imitating one of the indigenous species of Mayfly found in the rivers of the Eastern seaboard of the United States. As its name suggests, this nymph hails from the Catskills, where the adult insect is on the wing in late May.

Most fur-bodied nymphs are tied in this way, for instance, the Iron Blue and the Cahills.

Hooks: Down-eyed 10–12
Thread: Olive
Tail: Lemon Wood Duck
  fibres
Body: Greyish-brown fur
Ribbing: Fine gold wire
Wing-case: Light-grey goose
  or duck quill segment
Thorax: Greyish-brown fur
Hackle: Brown partridge
Head: Olive

1.
Take the thread down to the bend of the hook. Tie in some fibres of Wood Duck for the tail and a length of fine gold wire for the rib. Dub a greyish-brown fur onto the tying thread.

2.
Take the fur-dubbed thread back up the shank to form the abdomen. Follow this with the ribbing wire and, at this point, tie in a slip of grey goose or duck feather for the wing-case. Also, dub some fur to the tying thread.

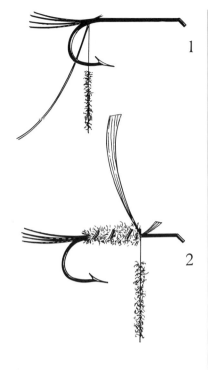

1

2

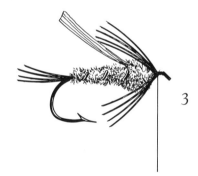

3

4

3.
Form a fur thorax and tie in a brown partridge hackle.

4.
Take the wing-case over the back. Form the head and finish the fly.

Chomper

This pattern was developed by Richard Walker, well-known British fly-fisherman and dresser. It can be dressed in many colours and should be fished slowly. It would appear to be more successful when used with a floating line and long leader and the sink-and-draw method is applied. When Walker tied it, it was not intended to resemble any particular natural, but depending on the colours used, it does actually look like a freshwater shrimp or a Corixa.

Hooks: Down-eyed 10–14
Thread: White, brown, olive, or
  black as desired for body colour
Body: Ostrich herl dyed to the
  colour required
Wing-case: Brown raffene
  (synthetic raffia)
Head: As thread

1.
Take the thread down to the bend of the hook, as usual. Give the thread a coating of varnish. When the varnish is dry, tie in at the bend a strip of brown raffene and two strands of ostrich herl.

2.
Take the thread back up the hook.

3.
Wind on the ostrich herl, tie off, and cut away the surplus.

4.
Dampen the raffene and stretch over the back in the "shell-back" style.

5.
Tie off and finish the fly in the usual way.

19

Collyer's Green

First tied by David Collyer to represent a nymph without actually endeavouring to copy a specific natural. They have been very successful throughout the world and have been responsible for some very large fish. The green (olive) is probably the most popular.

Hooks: Down-eyed 10–12
Thread: Olive
Body and Tail: Three strands olive-dyed goose or heron herl
Ribbing: Oval gold tinsel
Wing-case: Olive-dyed goose herl
Thorax: Olive-dyed ostrich herl
Head: Olive

Collyer's Brown

Hooks: Down-eyed 10–12
Thread: Brown (sherry spinner)
Body and Tail: Three strands cock-pheasant centre tail
Ribbing: Oval gold tinsel
Wing case: Cock-pheasant centre tail
Thorax: Chestnut-dyed ostrich herl
Head: Dark brown

Collyer's Grey

Hooks: Down-eyed 10–12
Thread: Black
Body and Tail: Undyed heron primary feathers
Ribbing: Oval silver tinsel
Thorax: Natural hen-ostrich herl (badger colour)
Head: Black

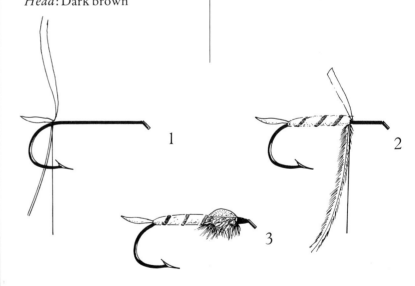

All the Collyer's Nymphs are tied in the same way. Only the colour is different.

1.
Take the thread down the hook as usual. At the bend, tie in a strip of dyed goose or heron herl with the tip projecting beyond the hook to act as a tail. At the same point tie in a length of oval gold tinsel.

2.
Return the thread down the shank. Follow this with the herl. Tie off but do not remove the excess feather (this will be used as the wing-case). Rib the body with the oval tinsel. Tie in a strip of ostrich herl in the appropriate colour.

3.
Wind on the ostrich herl to form the thorax; cut off excess. Take the goose feather over the ostrich herl and form the wing-case. Finish off as usual.

Corixa

Corixa

This nymph is one of the most popular in Europe. The natural Corixa is a small aquatic bug which feeds mostly on algae and vegetable matter and can be seen swimming swiftly to the surface to gather air. During this exercise, air becomes trapped on its abdomen which gives it a bright silver appearance which the trout find very attractive.

When fishing the artificial, it is most successful to fish it quite fast.

Hooks: Down-eyed 10–12
Thread: Brown
Body: White floss silk
Ribbing: Oval silver tinsel
Wing-case: Cock-pheasant
   tail fibres – two strands left
   as paddles
Throat Hackle (optional): Six
   fibres from a grouse hackle
Head: Brown

1.
Tie in a strip of cock-pheasant tail fibres and some oval silver tinsel at the bend of the hook.

2.
Take the tying thread back to the eye and tie in a length of floss silk.

3.
Form a body with the white silk. Tie off and rib with the tinsel.

4.
Take the cock-pheasant tail over the back, tie off, and trim excess fibres, leaving two fibres to form paddles.

5.
Finish the fly in the usual manner.

Sometimes a false hackle is tied in, but this is optional. This style of flytying is known as "shell back".

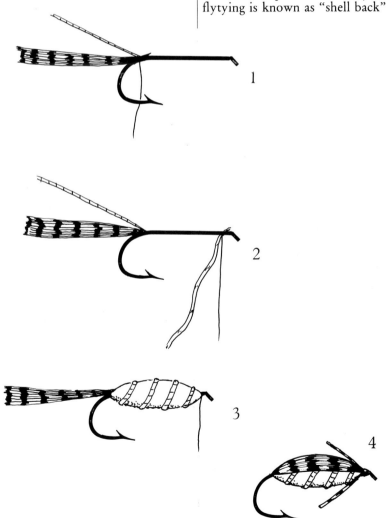

Damsel

This is the John Goddard dressing. A very popular and successful nymph.

The Damsel nymph is an easy pattern to tie when it represents the natural in the latter stages of its life cycle – when the mature nymph ascends to the surface and makes its way towards the bank where it can emerge and dry out and hatch into the adult. At this stage, the pattern can be dressed on a size 8 long-shanked hook and, using a floating line, fished just below the surface.

Hooks: Down-eyed 8–14
  long shank
Thread: Green
Tail: Tips of three olive cock
  hackles to extend three-
  eighths of an inch (1 cm)
  beyond the bend
Body: Medium olive seal's
  fur, tapering to tail for two-
  thirds of hook length
Ribbing: Gold wire
Thorax: Dark olive brown
  seal's fur
Wing-case: Brown mallard
  shoulder-feather fibres
Head: Dark green

1.

Wind thread down to the bend of the hook as normal, and then tie in the tail which comprises three hackle tips. At the same place, tie in a length of gold wire. Dub some medium olive seal's fur onto the tying thread.

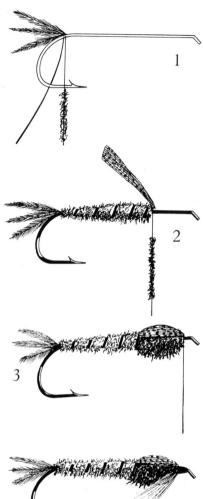

2.

Take thread up the hook forming a tapered body with the seal's fur. Rib with the gold wire, cut away any surplus ribbing, and then tie in a strip of brown mottled mallard. Dub on some dark olive seal's fur onto the tying thread.

3.

Form a thorax with the dark olive seal's fur and take the mallard feather over the back to form the wing-case.

4.

Tie in and wind on a small olive hen hackle and clip off all fibres above the hook.

Dragonfly Larva

This is the Taff Price dressing.

Hooks: Down-eyed 8–12
  long shank
Thread: Black
Tail: Spikey goose quill fibres
  dyed olive
Body: Mixed brown and
  green wool, brown pre-
  dominating
Ribbing: Yellow or green silk
Hackle: Brown partridge
Head: Peacock herl

1.

Tie in a length of green/brown mottled wool one-third of the way down the shank, continue the thread down the hook and, for the tail, tie in three goose quill fibres at the bend. At the same point, tie in a length of green or yellow silk for the ribbing medium.

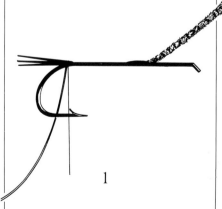

Golden Shrimp/ Olive Shrimp

Hook: Sedge hook, down-
    eyed 10–12
Thread: Yellow
Tail: Golden hackle fibres
Body: Golden yellow seal's
    fur (or substitute)
Ribbing: Gold oval tinsel
Hackle: Golden yellow cock
Back: Yellow raffene or natu-
    ral latex
Head: Yellow

1.
Take the thread to the bend of the hook, then wrap the shank with soft lead wire.

2.
Cover the wire with the tying thread and, for further strength, coat with clear varnish. Allow to dry and tie a few golden yellow hackle fibres in at the tail, a golden yellow hackle by the stalk, a strip of yellow raffene and the gold oval tinsel. Dub onto the tying thread some golden yellow seal's fur or substitute.

3.
Take the dubbed tying thread back toward the eye. Follow this with the hackle.

4.
Dampen the raffene and stretch over the back.

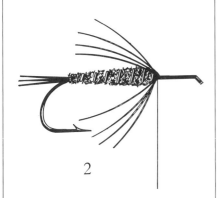

2

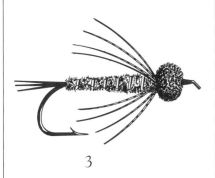

3

2.
Take the thread back to where the wool is tied in, take the wool down the shank and back again, followed by the rib. Cut off the surplus and tie in a brown partridge hackle.

3.
Tie in three strands of bronze peacock herl and wind around the shank to form a round head. Finish in the usual way.

5.
Take the ribbing and wind over the back and the body, taking care not to trap the hackle fibres. Finish the fly in the usual way. The raffene or latex can be left over the eye to form the tail of the shrimp, if wanted.

Olive shrimp is obtained by substituting olive materials for yellow.

Gold-ribbed Hare's Ear (American)

A highly successful pattern from the United States which has accounted for fish from all over the globe. It can be fished at any depth and can be dressed on a long- or a short-shank hook.

Hooks: Down-eyed 10–14, long or short shank
Thread: Black or brown
Tail: Hare's fur (the body fur is longer and more plentiful than the ear)
Body: Same as tail
Rib: Oval gold wire
Wing-case: Dyed black turkey tail or goose-wing quill
Thorax: The longest fibres of hare's body fur
Head: Black

1.
Tie in a bunch of hare's fur at the bend. Tie in gold wire and dub hare's ear fur onto the thread

2.
Wind the fur-dubbed thread up the shank. Follow with the gold rib and, at this point, tie in a slip of black dyed turkey or any black feather to form the wing-case. Dub on more fur for the thorax.

3.
Form the fur thorax and take the black feather over the back. Tie in, cut off the surplus feather, and complete the fly.

4.
The traditional British Gold-ribbed Hare's Ear as a nymph pattern.

5.
The Gold-ribbed Hare's Ear as a dry fly. Note the hare fur picked out to form the legs.

6.
The introduction of grey duck or starling gives a winged version.

Gold-ribbed Hare's Ear (British)

This differs from the American pattern in that it has no thorax.

1

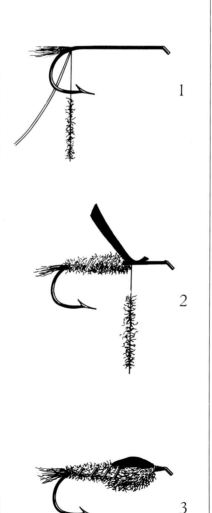

2

3

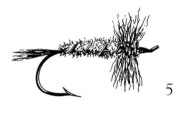

4

5

6

Hare Caddis

Hook: Down-eyed 10 long
   shank
Thread: Brown
Body: Brown seal's fur and
   the guard hairs of hare skin
   mixed
Ribbing: Copper wire
Wing-case: Cock-pheasant
   centre tail
Thorax: Pheasant herl
Hackle: Brown or medium-
   red hen hackle
Head: Brown

Hatching Sedge Pupa

This is the John Goddard dressing.

Hook: Down-eyed 12
Thread: Orange
Body: Orange seal's fur
Ribbing: Silver wire
Wing: Grey mallard wing-
   quill segments
Thorax: As body
Antennae: Two brown mal-
   lard fibres
Hackle: Brown partridge

The olive version is as above but
the seal's fur for the body and thorax
is olive-coloured and the hackle is
green-dyed grey partridge.

Hendrickson

This is tied in the same way as the
Catskill Hendrickson (*page 19*).
   Originally tied to imitate a Mayfly
native to the United States, *Ephemerella subvaria*, the Hendrickson
nymph is now becoming popular in
Europe.

Hook: Down-eyed 12–16
Thread: Olive
Tail: Wood Duck flank
Body: Grey/brown fur
Ribbing: Brown floss
Thorax: As body
Legs: Brown partridge
Wing-case: Dark brown
   turkey

Iron Blue Dun

Hooks: Down-eyed 14–16
Thread: Claret
Tail: White cock hackle fibres
Body: Mole fur
Hackle: Iron blue hen
Head: Claret

1.

Take the thread down to the bend of the hook and tie in the white cock hackle fibres which will form the tail.

2.

Dub the mole fur onto the thread and wind down the hook shank, so forming the body. Build it up towards the eye.

3.

Tie in the iron blue hen hackle (sparsely).

4.

Whip and varnish.

Light Cahill

This is the nymph of the famous Cahill dry fly originated by Dan Cahill of Port Jervis, New York. It is an imitation of the natural Mayfly (*Stenonema ithaca*) found extensively in the Eastern rivers of the United States. The Light Cahill is extremely effective all over Europe, both as a nymph and a dry fly. It is tied in the same manner as the Catskill Hendrickson (*page 19*).

Hooks: Down-eyed 10–14
   long shank
Thread: Cream or light
   brown
Tail: Three to four lemon
   Wood Duck fibres
Body: Light brown fur
Wing-case: Lemon Wood
   Duck
Thorax: As body
Hackle: Lemon Wood Duck
   fibres (divided on either side
   of the hook)

Mayfly (Collyer's pattern)

A pattern that is probably more successful on still water rather than on the river when the Mayfly hatch is on. On occasion, the trout probably take it for a Damsel or Dragonfly nymph. This is tied in the same way as the Damsel (*page 22*).

Hooks: Down-eyed 10 long
   shank
Thread: Olive
Tail: Three short strands of
   cock-pheasant centre-tail
   fibres
Body: Mixed olive and brown
   seal's fur
Ribbing: Gold wire
Wing-case: Hen-pheasant tail
Legs: Grey partridge breast
   feathers
Head: Olive

Below is a variation by Richard Walker.

Montana

As the name indicates, the fly is from Montana, the state with such great fishing rivers as the Yellowstone, the Big Hole, and the Missouri. It is becoming increasingly popular in Europe.

The nymph was tied to imitate the large larva of the Black Willow Stonefly. It could be that the trout take it for a large Dragonfly larva, who knows, but catch fish it does.

It is an easy nymph to tie and is often fished weighted.

Hooks: Down-eyed 8–10
  long shank
Thread: Black
Tail: Three black hackle tips
Body: Black chenille
Wing-case: Black chenille
Thorax: Yellow chenille
Hackle: Black hackle tied in
  through the thorax
Head: Black

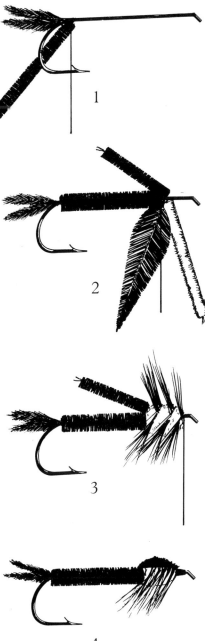

1.
At the bend, tie in three black hackle tips and a length of black chenille.

2.
Wind the chenille up the shank to form the body. Do not remove surplus as this will form the wing-case. At this point, tie in a black hackle and a length of yellow chenille.

3.
Take the thread to the eye and wind on the yellow chenille for the thorax; wind on the hackle.

4.
Take the chenille over the yellow thorax and tie off. Finish the fly in the usual way.

Mosquito Larva

A very popular nymph from the United States.

In general, stillwater trout usually preoccupy themselves with such food as the Chironomid midge and similar insects, but there are times when a rise of trout is brought on by the lowly mosquito.

Hooks: Down-eyed 14–16
Thread: Grey
Tail: Grizzle hackle fibres
Body: Grizzle saddle hackle
Feelers: Grizzle hackle fibres
  tied in over the eye
Thorax: Grizzle saddle
  hackle trimmed to shape

Olive Dun

Another broad-spectrum nymph pattern that imitates a wide variety of olive nymphs. It can be used on both still water and rivers. This kind of nymph is sold in tackle shops in great numbers and fits the bill when a nondescript olive is called for.

Hooks: Down-eyed 12–14
Thread: Brown
Tail: Three cock-pheasant tail fibres
Body: Olive seal's fur or a mixture of olive rabbit's fur and light muskrat fur (preferably from the animal's belly)
Ribbing: Gold
Wing-case: Grey goose quill or starling
Hackle: One turn of short olive hen's hackle
Head: Brown

Otter

A popular American and Canadian pattern, this is a broad-spectrum nymph used on streams and rivers. In Europe, otter fur is a somewhat scarce commodity but a similar coloured fur can be substituted.

Some fly dressers tie this fly with a thicker body, giving it a bushy appearance by dubbing it heavily and "picking out" the body with a dubbing needle.

The Otter is tied in the same way as the Catskill Hendrickson (*page 19*).

Hooks: Down-eyed 10–16
Thread: Black
Tail: Grey mallard flank fibres
Body: Otter fur
Wing-case: As tail
Thorax: Otter fur
Hackle: Grey mallard flank fibres – divided
Head: Black

Pheasant Tail

One could write a book on the subject of the pheasant-tail nymph alone. There are so many variants, every one with its own modification, that I shall endeavour to clarify the origins of the various patterns.

Frank Sawyer tied the first pheasant-tail nymph some thirty years ago on a short-shank hook which he used with great success for upstream nymphing. Its popularity soon found its way to the stillwater angler who set about modifying the nymph into countless patterns.

Years later, Arthur Cove tied his pattern also on the short-shank hook and dressed the nymph around the bend of the hook in the manner of the Buzzer (*page 18*), segmented the body with copper wire up to the thorax, which was rabbit's fur, and formed the wing-case with pheasant-tail fibres. The nymph was tied by Arthur Cove to imitate the large brown Buzzers found at Graffham.

Since then, the pheasant-tail nymph thorax has been substituted with all colours of seal's fur or chenille. It has grown tails, legs, full hackles, changed its copper wire for gold or silver, been tied on long-shanked hooks, and, finally, been weighted. I have given both Sawyer's and Cove's dressings.

Sawyer's
Hooks: Down-eyed 10–16 short shank
Thread: Brown
Tail: Tips of the cock-pheasant tail fibres used for the body
Body: Cock-pheasant tail fibres
Ribbing: Copper wire
Wing-case: As body
Head: Brown

This method is slightly different from that which Frank Sawyer used, but it is the way I prefer (Frank Sawyer used the copper wire as a tying thread).

Sawyer's Pheasant Tail

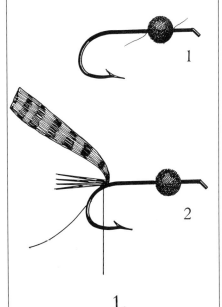

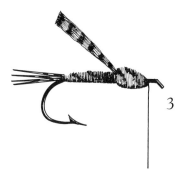

1.

Using fine copper wire, form a ball at the point where the thorax comes on the hook.

2.

Take tying thread to the bend of the hook and, at this point, tie in a few tips of cock-pheasant tail fibres to form the actual tail of the fly. The rest is used for the body. Tie in a length of fine copper wire.

3.

Twist the copper wire and the pheasant-tail fibres together and wind up the hook until you come to the copper-wire ball. Tie in an extra length of pheasant-tail fibres and leave for the time being. Continue to wind the original copper-wire/ pheasant-tail fibres until the copper-wire thorax is covered. Tie off and cut off the surplus.

4.

Take the bunch of cock-pheasant tail fibres over the thorax to form the wing-case. Finish off in the usual way.

Cove's Pheasant Tail

Cove's

> *Hooks*: Down-eyed 8–14
> short shank
> *Thread*: Brown
> *Body*: Cock-pheasant tail
> fibres
> *Ribbing*: Copper wire, or
> silver and gold
> *Thorax*: Rabbit under-fur
> mixed with a few guard hairs
> *Wing-case*: Cock-pheasant
> tail fibres

1.

Tie in a bunch of cock-pheasant tail fibres and a length of oval gold tinsel at the point on the hook shown.

2.

Take the tying thread down around the hook shank, covering the feather fibres and ribbing.

3.

Take tying thread back up the hook shank, about two-thirds of the length. Follow with the pheasant tail and rib with the oval tinsel. Trim off the surplus and, at this point, tie in a further bunch of pheasant-tail fibres for the wing-case. Dub some rabbit or hare fur onto the tying thread.

4.

Wind on the fur to form the thorax. Take the wing-case over. Finish the fly in the usual way.

5.

Variations of this nymph are legion. Fig. 5 shows a long-shank version with a tail. The thorax fur can be any fur material and any colour desired.

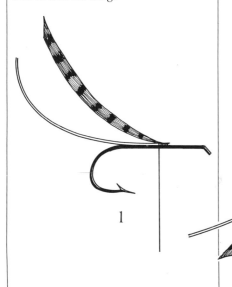

1

2

3

4

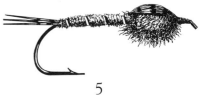

5

Sedge Pupa

Probably one of John Goddard's most famous patterns, this was originally tied by him in the late 1950s to imitate the pupal stage of the Sedge found in great numbers in the stomachs of the trout at Blagdon and Chew.

Most effective from midsummer onwards. This pattern is tied in four basic colours: orange, green, brown, or cream. The orange pattern is illustrated.

> *Hooks*: Down-eyed 10–12 long shank
> *Thread*: Brown
> *Body*: Orange, green, brown or cream seal's fur (whichever colour is required); a little fluorescent floss silk may be wound sparsely over the orange or green fur
> *Ribbing*: Narrow silver tinsel
> *Thorax*: Dark brown condor herl or dyed turkey (light brown with brown body)
> *Wing-case*: Strip of pale coloured feather fibre
> *Hackle*: Hen hackle tied sparsely, 1½ – 2 turns
> *Head*: Brown

1.
At the bend of the hook, tie in a length of narrow silver tinsel. Dub seal's fur of the desired colour onto the thread.

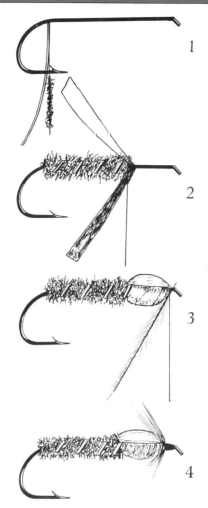

1
2
3
4

2.
Take the thread two-thirds of the way up the hook shank and rib the fur body with even turns of the silver tinsel. Now tie in a pale brown condor herl or dyed goose herl for the wing-case and a strip of dark brown condor herl to form the thorax.

3.
Form the thorax by wrapping the dark herl around the hook shank; take the lighter herl over the back to form the wing-case. Cut away any surplus herl and tie in a honey hen hackle.

4.
Wind on the hackle and complete the fly.

Slate-wing Olive

This pattern represents the nymph of the Ephemerid (*Ephemerella flavilinea*), another of the American species of Mayfly. Large hatches of this insect are to be found on many of the Montana rivers such as the Snake and the Yellowstone. They are to be found mainly in the faster stretches of the river. The pattern is tied in the same way as the Catskill Hendrickson (*page 19*).

> *Hooks*: Down-eyed 12–14
> *Thread*: Olive
> *Tail*: Three Canada Goose quill fibres
> *Body*: Brownish-grey fur
> *Rib*: Grey silk or floss
> *Wing-case*: Canada Goose quill segment
> *Thorax*: As body
> *Hackle*: Medium-dun hen
> *Head*: Olive

Stick Fly

This pattern comes in many variants and supposedly represents the Caddis larva in its case. It can be very effective.

> *Hooks*: Down-eyed 8–10 long shank
> *Thread*: Brown (or black)
> *Tail*: Two – three golden pheasant's tippet
> *Body*: Peacock herl wound thinly
> *Hackle*: Sparsely tied short red cock hackle
> *Head*: Brown (or black)

1.

Tie in a few strands of golden pheasant-tippet fibres at the bend. At the same point, tie in three or four strands of peacock herl.

2.

Return the tying thread back along the hook and follow with the peacock herl to form a slim body. Tie off and cut away the surplus. Tie in a short stiff hackle (usually natural red but this is not important).

3.

Wind on the hackle and finish off the fly.

4.

Another type of stick fly has no tail but has a fluorescent silk thorax which is very often fluorescent green. The silver rib is optional.

Stonefly Creeper

The Stoneflies of America are numerous and their colours legion. On the latest assessments, they number somewhere between 400 and 500. They feed on vegetation and are found in running water. The average life cycle is twelve months, and it is a matter of interest that large concentrations of Stonefly nymphs denude the rivers of Mayfly nymphs through predation. They can grow to a length of 2–3 inches (5-7 cm) in the West. The larger hatches are seen in the spring and early summer. This is probably one of the more popular Stonefly patterns used.

> *Hooks*: Down-eyed 8–12 long shank
> *Thread*: Yellow
> *Tail*: Dark cock-pheasant centre-tail fibres
> *Wing-case*: Barred Wood Duck flank feathers
> *Body (Abdomen)*: Stripped ginger hackle quill
> *Thorax*: Amber African goat or substitute
> *Legs*: Brown partridge hackle
> *Head*: Yellow

1.

At the bend, tie in two strands of dark cock-pheasant tail fibres, a strip of Wood Duck flank (or substitute), and a stripped hackle quill.

2.

Take the thread halfway up the shank and follow this with the hackle quill to form the abdomen of the fly. Dub some amber fur onto the thread.

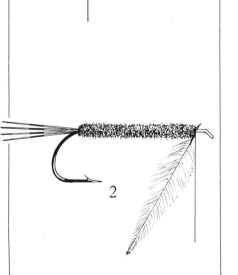

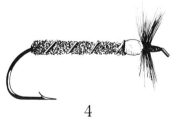

Stonefly Creeper

Taddy

A very popular fly, used a lot in South Africa and one of those patterns that is very easy to tie and easy to imitate the natural with. The Tadpole is found throughout the world in its various forms and is best emulated in the spring. Some advocate fishing the Taddy on a long leader with a slow sinker or medium density line. Others, especially the South Africans, use it as a dropper with a small lure (for example, the Walker's Killer) on the point with great effect.

> *Hooks*: Down-eyed 10–14
> *Thread*: Black
> *Tail*: Dyed black squirrel
> *Body*: Tying thread
> *Head*: Black

1.

This is a simple version of a very effective fly. At the bend tie in a bunch of black hair. Squirrel is ideal.

2.

With the tying thread, form a rotund body. Finish the fly with a whip finish.

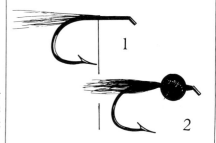

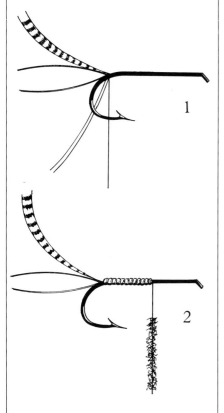

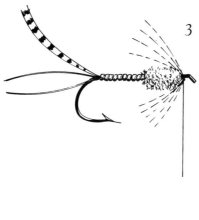

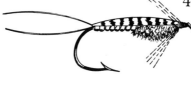

3.

Form the thorax of the fly with the amber fur and wind on a partridge hackle, collar style.

4.

Take the strip of Wood Duck over the back and tie off. This separates the hackle. Finish the fly with a neat head.

Ted's Stonefly

This nymph, designed by Ted Trueblood, is tied in the same way as the Montana and the numbers below refer to the step-by-step illustrations for the Montana (*page 27*).

Hooks: Down-eyed 8–12
  long shanked
Thread: Black
Tail: Two red/brown goose-
  quill fibres
Body: Brown chenille
Wing-case: Brown chenille
Thorax: Orange chenille
Hackle: Black hackle pal-
  mered over the thorax
Head: Black

1.
Take the thread down the hook to the bend and tie in two red/brown goose-quill fibres. At the same place, tie in a length of brown chenille.

2.
Wind the brown chenille up the shank to form the body. Do not remove the surplus as this will form the wing-case. At this point, tie in a black hackle and the orange chenille.

3.
Take the black thread to the eye and wind on the orange chenille to form the thorax. Wind on the hackle.

4.
Take the brown chenille over the orange thorax and tie off and finish the fly in the usual way.

Tellico

This pattern originated in the southern United States and in the last few years has found popularity in Britain and parts of Europe. Usually fished weighted.

Hooks: Down-eyed 8–14
  long shank
Thread: Black
Tail: Speckled Gallina
  (guinea fowl) fibres
Wing-case: Cock-pheasant
  tail feather fibres
Body: Yellow floss or wool
Ribbing: Peacock herl
Hackle: Ginger or honey
  hackle
Head: Black

1.
For the tail, tie in a few fibres of black and white guinea-fowl hackle, together with one strand of peacock herl and a strip of cock-pheasant tail for the back.

2.
Take the tying thread back up the shank and tie in a length of yellow floss or wool.

3.
Form the body by winding the floss down the hook and back again. Remove surplus floss. Rib the body with the peacock herl and then take the cock-pheasant feather over the back, tie off, and cut away surplus feathers.

4.
Wind on a light ginger or honey hackle, collar style, and finish the fly in the usual manner.

Tellico

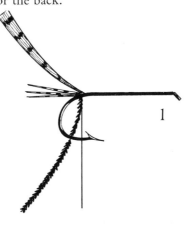

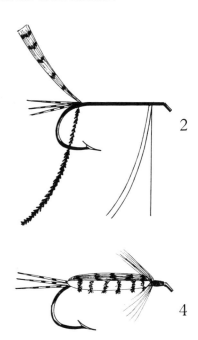

Walker's Longhorn Sedge Pupa

Sometimes mistakenly represented. The Sedge pupa is in effect a hatching adult, because the actual pupa is quiescent. The pattern can be tied in a variety of colours, such as green or amber.

Hooks: Down-eyed 10–14
Thread: Brown or olive
Body: Rear two-thirds green
 or amber ostrich herl,
 twisted and wound thick
 and ribbed with fine gold
 thread; front-one third sepia
 ostrich herl
Hackle: Brown partridge
Horns: Two strands of long
 cock-pheasant tail fibres,
 twice as long as the hook
Head: Brown

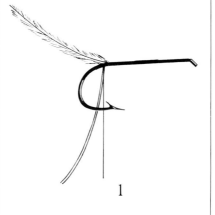

1

2

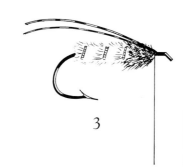

3

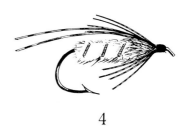

4

1.
At the bend, tie in a strand or two of ostrich herl (amber or green) and a length of oval gold tinsel.

2.
Take the thread two-thirds of the way up the shank of the hook. Follow with the ostrich herl and then the rib. Cut off the surplus herl and rib. Tie in one or two strands of sepia ostrich herl.

3.
Take the thread back towards the eye and then wind on the sepia ostrich herl to form the thorax. Cut off surplus herl. Tie in the two strands of cock-pheasant tail for the horns.

4.
Finally, wind on a brown partridge hackle and then complete the fly with a neat head.

Wonder Nymph

An • American pattern which in Europe is normally weighted. Fished slow on the bottom, it can induce some savage takes.

Hooks: Down-eyed 6–12
  long shank
Thread: Black
Tail: Black porcupine bristles
  (moose mane can substitute)
Body: Dubbed muskrat fur
Rib: Blue dun and brown
  hackle wrapped together
  (clip hackle to the required
  length, usually one-eighth
  inch or 3 mm)
Head: Black ostrich herl

1.

Take thread down the hook to the bend and tie in three porcupine bristles or moose mane for the tail. At the same point, tie in a blue dun

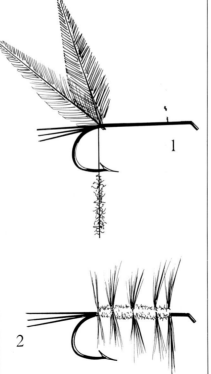

and brown cock hackle. Dub muskrat fur onto the tying thread.

2.

Wind the dubbed thread back up the shank. Follow this by winding the two cock hackles together. Tie off and cut off the excess.

3.

Clip down the hackles and tie in some black ostrich herl for the head. Finish fly as usual.

Zug Bug

A popular American nymph, also known as the Davis Special or Kemp's bug, which has become very popular in Britain during the last few years.

Hooks: Down-eyed 10–14
Thread: Black
Tail: Three peacock sword tips; length about two-thirds of body
Body: Bronze peacock herl
Ribbing: Silver tinsel
Wing-case: Barred lemon Wood Duck fibres tied in at the front, length about one-third of body; (substitute: dyed grey mallard)
Hackle: Two turns of soft long furnace tied on as a collar and tied back; (brown hen sometimes preferred)
Head: Black

1.
At the bend, tie in three or four strands of peacock sword tips for the tail. At the same point, tie three or four strands of bronze peacock herl and a strip of silver tinsel for the rib.

2.
Wind the bronze peacock herl up the hook shank to form the body. Follow with the rib.

3.
On top of the hook, tie in a few fibres of Wood Duck or substitute (dyed grey mallard). Beneath the hook, a few fibres of brown hen hackle are tied in as the hackle. Some flytiers prefer a collar-style hackle. Finish the fly with a neat head.

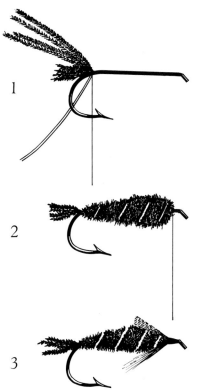

A scene at the oldest and probably one of the most attractive still waters in Great Britain, Blagdon. Some anglers wade unnecessarily. This one is striving for distance, and his efforts have produced a poor back cast. However, he had a good day's fishing and caught six fine rainbows, all of them on the Muddler Minnow.

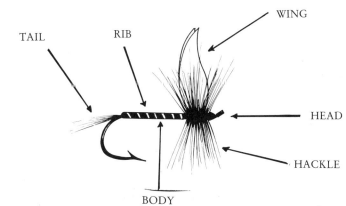

The dry fly is meant to imitate any fly that floats on the surface of the water. It might be a terrestrial, such as the common black ant or beetle, that has been blown onto the surface of the water. It might be a newly hatched adult, lying on the surface waiting for its wings to dry, or it might be a spent fly that has just laid its eggs on the surface and is dying or already dead. Flies lie very delicately on the water and it is the flytier's job to tie an artificial that will imitate them.

The art of dry-fly fishing consists basically of presenting your fly so that it settles on the surface of the water just as delicately as the natural, so that it floats well, properly cocked, into the view of the unsuspecting fish. The well-dressed dry fly will have all the qualities necessary to float well and realistically. This is where the choice of materials is important. The hackle, chosen from the cock, should have superior floating qualities; its stiffness enables the fly to sit properly on the surface of the water. The hook is lightweight and up-eyed, specially designed for dry flies, and is dressed with the right balance to give the fly the correct behaviour on the water.

In most cases, stealth is essential when approaching a rise. Sometimes, there is nothing else for it but to get down on your hands and knees, and crawl into position for your cast, always remembering to keep your rod top from waving about above the skyline or in the trout's line of vision, which is enlarged considerably by the refraction of the light at the surface. Once the desired position is reached, cast your fly well above (a couple of yards or metres) the trout's last noted position and let the fly float downstream into the trout's range of vision, with the minimum of surface interference. If the trout rises to your fly and you miss the strike, allow the fly to float on down the river before lifting off, false casting, and laying it on again upstream. It is surprising how often the trout will have another go at the fly, more or less straight away. However, do not continue to bombard the same fish for long. Move on to the next rise.

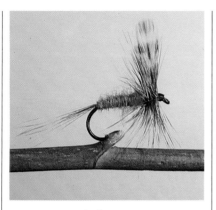

Adams

An American pattern fished with great effect around May when the Medium Olive is hatching off in great numbers. It is tied in the same way as the Light Hendrickson (*page 53*).

Hooks: Up-eyed 14–16
Thread: Black
Tail: Grizzle hackle
Body: Grey dubbing
Wings: Grizzle hackle points
Hackle: Mixed grizzle and
  brown
Head: Black

Aurlandsfluen
(Aurland Fly)

This is a sea-trout dry fly from Scandinavia, named after the Aurland river, a fast-flowing water that runs into Sognefjord in Norway.

Hooks: Up-eyed 10
Thread: Lemon
Tail: Twenty–thirty long stiff
  light brown hackle fibres
Body: Lemon silk or wool
Hackle: Three long and stiff
  light brown saddle hackle
  feathers covering ½ of the
  hook shank
Head: Lemon, varnished
  with clear varnish

Badger Hackle

Hooks: Up-eyed 12
Thread: Black
Tail: Black cock-hackle fibres
Body: Black floss
Ribbing: Silver wire
Hackle: Well-marked badger
  hackle, i.e., with a dark
  centre
Head: Black

Beacon Beige

A pattern first tied by a member of the Wills family of Dulverton in 1917 and called the Beige. The original dressing was altered somewhat in the late 1940s by Peter Deane, whose window overlooked the Culmstock Beacon in the Culm Valley; hence the pattern became known as the Beacon Beige. A very popular fly in Devon.

Bi-Visible

Hooks: Up-eyed 14–16
Thread: Light brown
Tail: Four strong fibres of
Plymouth Rock cock hackle
Body: Stripped peacock eye
quill
Hackle: Dark red Indian
game and grizzle cock
hackle
Head: Brown

1.

Take the light brown thread down
the shank to the bend of the hook
and tie in the four fibres of Plymouth Rock cock hackle to form the
tail. Tie them pointing slightly
down. Then tie in the stripped
peacock.

2.

Take the thread back down the
shank and varnish.

3.

While the varnish is still wet wind on
the stripped peacock to form the
body and tie in. Then select the dark
red Indian game and well-marked
grizzle hackles and wind on.

4.

Finish in the usual way.

Bi-Visible

There are many variants of this
pattern: badger, brown, blue dun,
black, furnace, ginger, grizzle, olive
and pink lady. With the exception of
the pink lady, these patterns are
often tied with embossed tinsel
bodies. The pattern is attributed to
Edward Hewitt. The black pattern is
given here.

Hooks: Up-eyed 10–16
Thread: Black
Tail: Black hackle fibres or
hackle tips
Hackle: Black hackle palmered over the body with
2/3 turns of white hackle
tied in at the eye
Head: Black

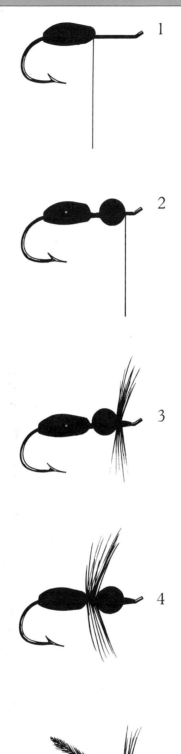

Black Ant

This is a simple and effective ant pattern. During the hot weather of the late summer, the ants appear in large numbers and, if the wind takes them over the water, they often fall onto the surface to be gorged by the trout.

Hooks: Up-eyed 14–16
Thread: Black
Body: Black silk (tied ant-like)
Wings: Grey hackle points
Hackle: Black cock
Head: Black

1.
Take the black thread down the hook and form the abdomen with it.

2.
Form the thorax in the same way, leaving a slight gap between it and the abdomen.

3.
Now wind on a black cock hackle.

4.
As an alternative, you can wind the hackle after the abdomen and before the thorax.

5.
For a winged version, two grey hackle points are tied in before winding the hackle.

Black Gnat

The Black Gnat is a common fly in most parts. The first tying of this pattern could well have originated in the Usk valley where the Gnat can be seen in clouds. Very often, the Gnats fall onto the water while still paired, so they are helpless, and the waiting trout gorge themselves. I have, for this reason, included the dressing for a mating pair below.

Hooks: Up-eyed 16
Thread: Black
Body: Layers of black silk or dyed black swan, goose, or ostrich herl
Ribbing (optional): Silver wire
Wing: Grey duck
Hackle: Black cock
Head: Black

1.
At the point shown, tie in two slips of grey duck upright. Take the thread down the hook shank. Tie in a length of silver wire at the bend.

2.
Form the body of the fly with the tying thread (for larger sizes, you can use floss silk). After forming the body, wind on the ribbing.

3.
Tie in a black hackle behind the wing and wind around the hook shank. Finish off the fly with a whip finish and varnish.

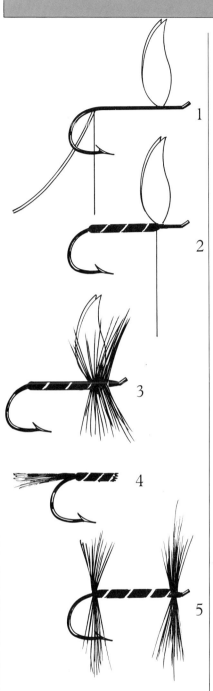

1

2

3

4

5

Cinnamon Sedge

An imitation of one of the larger Sedges that starts to hatch off at midsummer and becomes prolific on the water some weeks later. A fly that prefers the latter end of the day. It is also an excellent pattern for sea trout.

Hooks: Up-eyed 10–14
Thread: Brown
Body: Cock pheasant tail
  fibres
Ribbing: Fine gold wire
Wing: Cinnamon hen quill
Hackle: Palmered ginger
  cock

4.

A version with a tail.

5.

The mating Black Gnat or mating Black Midge looks like this. First a hackle is tied in at the bend. Then come, as above, the body, the ribbing, and, finally, another hackle at the head.

Blue Winged Olive

An excellent fly on chalk streams. The natural first appears in the late spring and continues throughout the season into the first frosts. It is larger than the Iron Blue or Pale Watery duns.

In the imago, or adult, stage, both sexes are known to all fly fishermen as sherry spinners.

Hooks: Up-eyed 12
Thread: Black
Tag: Flat gold
Tail: Pale dun cock
Body: Greenish-olive seal's
  fur
Hackle: Medium olive
Wings: Darkest starling
Head: Black

Coachman

A popular pattern that bears no resemblance to any natural insect. It can be finished wet or dry. Its name is generally thought to come from a coachman by the name of Tom Bosworth who worked for three British sovereigns: George IV, William IV, and Queen Victoria. It is said that he tied the pattern with the materials he had at his disposal when at a loss one evening to raise a fish. In any event, its popularity has increased over the years and it is now recognized as a standard pattern, being very popular in North America.

Hooks: Up-eyed 10–16
Thread: Black
Body: Bronze peacock herl
Hackle: Ginger cock
Wings: White duck or goose
Head: Black

1.

Cover the hook shank with the tying thread in the usual way and return the thread to the point shown. At this point, tie in two slips of white duck quill and tie in upright as for normal dry flies.

2.

Take thread down to the bend and tie in about four strands of bronze peacock herl.

3.

Return the thread back to behind the wing and form the body of the fly by

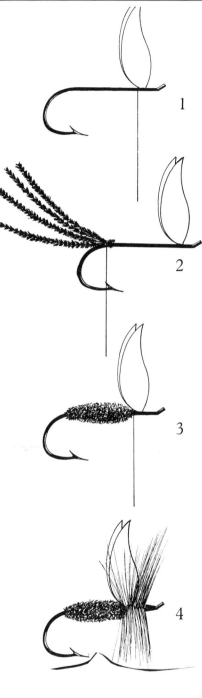

creating a rope out of the herl and wrapping it around the hook. Cut off the surplus herl.

4.

Wind on a hackle and tie it in just behind the wing and wound to the front. Finish the fly with a whip finish.

Coch Y Bondhu

A traditional Welsh beetle pattern. Can be fished wet or dry.

Hooks: Up-eyed 12–14
  (Down-eyed for wet)
Thread: Black
Tag: Fine flat gold tinsel (or lurex)
Body: 4 or 5 peacock herls
Hackle: Coch y Bondhu
  (cock for dry fly, hen for wet fly)

1.

At the bend, tie in a strip of flat gold tinsel and four or five fibres of peacock herl.

2.

Wrap the gold tinsel around the hook to form a gold tip, tie off, and remove the surplus tinsel. Take the thread back down the hook, form the body by wrapping the herl around the thread, cut off surplus herl. Tie in a well-marked dark furnace (Coch y Bondhu) hackle by the stalk.

3.

Wind on the hackle and complete the fly in the usual way.

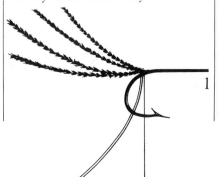

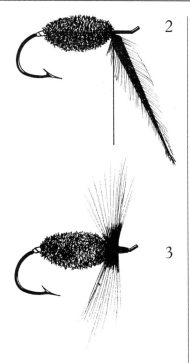

Crane Fly

Hooks: Up-eyed 10–12 long
  shank
Thread: Sherry spinner
Body: 4-6 cinnamon turkey
  herl or latex
Legs: 6 cock-pheasant centre-
  tail fibres (knotted)
Wings: Light red or ginger
  cock-hackle points (tied
  spent)
Hackle: Light red or ginger
  cock
Head: Brown (or black)

1.

Prepare six cock-pheasant tail fibres by knotting the actual fibres in two places (these are to simulate the jointed legs of the natural insect).

2.

Take the thread to the bend and tie in a strip of cinnamon-coloured turkey wing quill or latex.

3.

Return the thread up the hook shank to point shown. Wind on the turkey herl or latex to form the body.

4.

Tie in the knotted cock-pheasant fibres beneath the hook.

5.

Tie in two light red or ginger cock hackles tied spent.

6.

Wind on a light red or ginger cock hackle. Finish off the fly as usual.

Crane Fly
(Daddy Long-Legs)

A Richard Walker pattern that accounts for many fish. The "Daddy" tempts the bigger fish from the bottom and if sufficient numbers of the fly are being blown onto the water there is a frenzy of feeding. If you have not got the pattern in your fly box you will have a very lean time. The natural "Daddy" is very often dapped in the "loch style" type of fishing and does kill large numbers of fish. If, however, you are fishing one of the many reservoirs that have great numbers of this insect on the water, it is probably best fished "still", that is to say, cast out and left floating until the trout comes along and sucks it down. Do allow a little time for the fish to turn before setting the hook. There are two tyings for the body, the first being cinnamon turkey herl and the second a latex body.

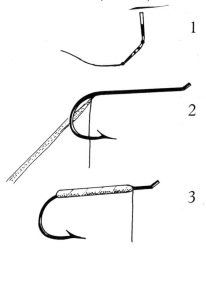

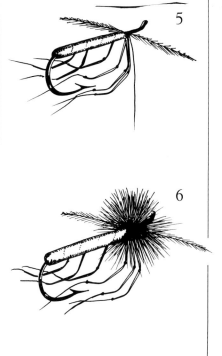

Dave's Hopper

Dark Cahill

This is tied in the same way as the Light Cahill (*page 52*).

Hooks: Up-eyed 12–16
Thread: Light brown
Tail: Brown hackle fibres
Body: Muskrat or equivalent
fine brown fur
Hackle: Medium red goose
Wings: Wood Duck (upright
and divided)
Head: Brown

Dave's Hopper

Tied by Dave Whitlock and a very popular pattern in the United States. Some dressers apply varnish to the wings to make them stronger.

Hooks: Up-eyed 6–14
Thread: Brown
Tail: Natural tan-grey deer
body (or bucktail) hair dyed
red and loop of yellow body
yarn
Ribbing: Brown hackle

Body: Yellow yarn
Underwing: Yellow bucktail
Overwing: Brown mottled
turkey-wing slips
Head: Spun deer body. Leave
a few natural tips extended
on each side. The head
should be wide and flat

1.
At the bend, tie in a bunch of red-dyed deer body hair or bucktail, a length of yellow wool, and a brown hackle.

2.
Form a loop with the yellow wool (this is an addition to the red tail). Take the rest of the wool up the hook shank to form the body. Follow with the hackle, palmer-style.

3.
Clip the hackle as in the drawing and tie in some yellow bucktail.

4.
Flank the yellow hair with slips of mottled turkey wing and start to spin the deer-hair head (see Muddler Minnow, page 111).

5.
Complete the deer-hair spinning and clip to shape, leaving some fibres unclipped as a hackle. Finish off the fly in the usual manner.

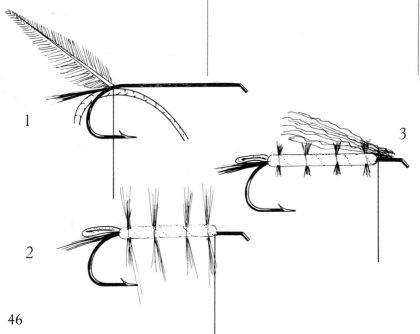

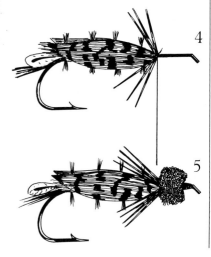

French Partridge Mayfly

Hooks: Up-eyed 10 long
  shank
Thread: Black or brown
Tail: Bunch of cock-pheasant
  centre-tail fibres
Body: Natural raffia
Ribbing: Black silk, red silk,
  or gold wire
Hackle: Inner natural red
  cock. Outer French par-
  tridge (optional palmered
  with olive cock)
Head: Black or brown

3.

Wind the hackle, palmer-style, back to the bend and secure with the ribbing medium. Take the rib down the body, securing the turns of hackle as you do so.

4.

Tie in a striped French partridge hackle by the tip and wind on. Finish the fly with a neat head.

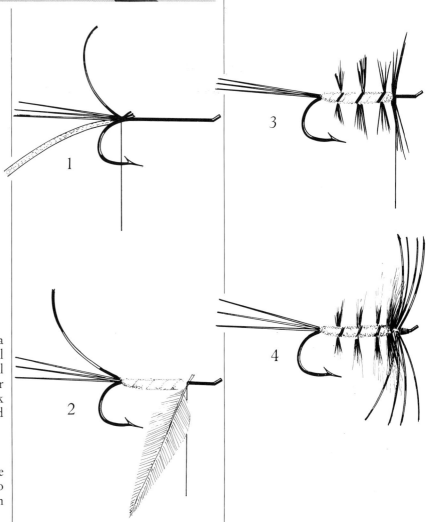

1.

At the bend of the hook, tie in a bunch of cock-pheasant centre-tail fibres for the tail, a strip of natural raffia and either a length of black or red silk or gold wire (I prefer black silk, but other patterns call for red silk and some gold wire).

2.

Take the tying thread back up the hook and follow up with the raffia to form the body. At this point, tie in an olive hackle.

G. & H. Sedge

A very good pattern first tied by John Goddard and Cliff Henry, the G. and H. being the initials of their surnames.

It is a very versatile pattern and can be fished in many situations from the bank, used as a dropper from the boat, or skipped across the surface of the water. Deer hair has the asset of being extremely buoyant.

It has become very popular in the United States. It is not the easiest of patterns to tie.

Hooks: Up-eyed 10 −12 long shank
Thread: Brown
Body: Deer hair
Underbody: Green or yellow wool (dubbed seal's fur, if preferred)
Hackle: Red cock
Head: Brown

1.

Tie in at the bend a length of green or yellow wool. The original pattern called for a dubbed seal's fur body, but this way is somewhat easier.

2.

Spin deer hair onto the hook shank, as for the Muddler Minnow head (page 111).

3.

Clip the deer hair to shape as shown and take the length of wool under the hook and tie off (this represents

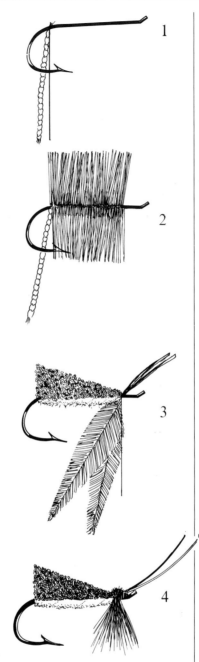

the abdomen of the caddis). Tie in two natural red cock hackles (do not cut off stalks).

4.

Wind on the hackles, clip off the top hackle fibres, form the head of the fly, and leave the hackle stalks as antennae.

Ginger Quill

A good variation to its cousin the Red Quill and used to imitate the Pale Watery and Light Olive Dun. Tie as the Quill Gordon (page 57). Above is the unwinged version, below the winged.

Hooks: Up-eyed 14 −16
Thread: Tan
Tail: Pale-brown ginger
Body: Pale peacock quill
Hackle: Pale-brown ginger
Wings: Palest starling
Head: Brown

Ginger Quill (winged)

Grannom

First tied by Pat Russell, this pattern is an early-season fly. The female appears to be the favourite for the trout and is distinguished by the green egg-sac that she carries after mating. The fly is tied in the same way as the Green Peter *(right)*.

This is predominantly a dry fly but there is a wet version which can be very successful.

Hooks: Up-eyed 14
Thread: Bright green
Body: Fur from the base of a hare's ear, spun on brown silk
Egg-sac: A short length of either green wool or floss at the tail end
Wings: Hen-pheasant wing feather
Hackle: Greyish-brown hackle

Green Drake Mayfly

Hooks: Up-eyed 10 long shank
Thread: Brown
Tail: Three cock-pheasant tail fibres
Body: Light olive plastic raffia
Wings: Mallard drake breast feather dyed green and cut to shape
Hackle: Yellowish-green cock
Head: Brown

(below) This photograph of the Green Drake Mayfly shows the spread of the wings.

Green Peter

A very popular fly for fishing big trout on the Irish lakes, the Green Peter resembles a Sedge that swims on the surface to the shore. Some dressings call for a palmered hackle.

Hooks: Up-eyed 12 –14
Thread: Olive
Body: Olive seal's fur
Wing: Bronze mallard
Ribbing: Fine gold wire
Hackle: Dark ginger cock
Head: Olive

1.
Take the olive tying thread down to the bend of the hook.

2.
Dub on the olive seal's fur.

3.
Wind back up the shank to form the body. Follow with the ribbing.

4.
Tie in the bronze mallard for the wing, to lie down well over the body, "sedge-like".

5.
Tie in the dark ginger cock hackle and wind on over the base of the wing. Finish in the usual way.

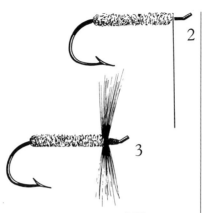

Grey Wulff

Grey Duster

A traditional Welsh fly that can be used throughout the season. Excellent on rough water and certainly a pattern to have in your box during a *Caenis* hatch. It can usually be seen on broken water and its buoyancy is excellent. An easy fly to tie.

> *Hooks*: Up-eyed 12–14
> *Thread*: Black
> *Body*: Grey fur
> *Hackle*: Well-marked badger hackle
> *Head*: Black

1.
Take the thread to the bend of the hook and dub on the fur mixture.

2.
Form the body by winding the fur-laden thread back up the hook.

3.
Wind on a well-marked badger hackle and complete the fly in the usual way.

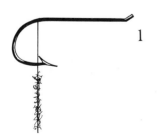

Grey Wulff

An American fly invented in the 1930s by Lee Wulff who extensively used animal hair for his patterns. Today, the practice is commonplace and the method of tying is identical. It catches many fish in very different surroundings and is used very successfully as an imitation of Mayfly. Its buoyancy is excellent. The inventor originally used elk hair for the wings and tail but today bucktail, squirrel, or calftail can be used very satisfactorily. The variants include White, Brown, and Royal Wulff.

> *Hooks*: Up-eyed 8–14
> *Thread*: Black
> *Tail*: Brown elk, bucktail, squirrel, or calftail
> *Body*: Mole or grey fur or wool
> *Wings*: As for tail, tied forward
> *Hackle*: Grey cock
> *Head*: Black

1.
Tie in a bunch of fine brown bucktail on top of the hook, raise upright, and divide in two by means of a figure-of-eight whipping. These are the wings.

2.
Take the thread down to the bend, covering the butt ends of the hair. Tie in a few fibres of bucktail at the bend to form the tail. Also tie in here a length of grey wool.

3.
Wind the wool up the hook to form the body. Wind on a grey hackle behind and in front of the wings, and finish in the usual way.

Iron Blue Dun

There have been many patterns tied of the Iron Blue since the middle of the eighteenth century. It is a very prolific fly found on fast and slow moving waters. After forty-eight hours as an adult, it changes into the Jenny Spinner.

There are many variations. The following is David Collyer's.

Hooks: Up-eyed 12–14
Thread: Crimson
Tail: Two white cock-hackle fibres
Body: Dark heron herl
Ribbing: Olive silk
Hackle: Dark-blue dun cock

1.

Take the crimson tying thread down to the bend and tie in the two white cock-hackle fibres which will form the tail.

2.

At the same point, tie in two strands of dark heron herl and wind around the shank down towards the eye, stopping just short.

3.

Follow down with the olive silk ribbing.

4.

Tie in the hackle and finish in the usual way.

If you wish to wing the fly add a dark-dyed starling wing.

Kite's Imperial

Oliver Kite first tied this fly in 1960. Along with the Olive Quill and the Rough Olive, it is tied to imitate the large Dark Olive. Basically, the Dark Olive is an early-season fly, but this is an excellent pattern to keep in your fly box at all times.

Hooks: Up-eyed 14–16
Thread: Purple
Tail: Grey/brown hackle fibres (later in the season use honey dun)
Body: Heron herl
Ribbing: Gold wire
Thorax: Heron herl
Hackle: Honey dun cock hackle (light ginger if preferred)

1.

At the bend, tie in a few grey/brown hackle fibres for the tail (this colour is for the early season; later, honey dun hackle fibres are used). At the same point, tie in a strip of heron herl (about three strands) and a length of fine gold wire.

2.

Wind the herls down the body. Follow with the gold wire ribbing. With the ends of the herl form a thorax by doubling back the feather fibre. Clip off excess materials and tie in a honey dun cock hackle (some use light ginger).

3.

Complete the fly.

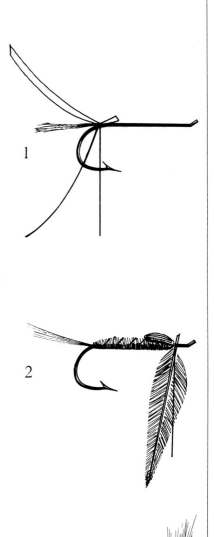

Lake Olive

One of the few dry fly patterns that is well worth having in your box when fishing large still waters when there is a hatch of the Pond or Lake Olive. Neither comes off in large numbers but, if you are fortunate enough to be in the vicinity of a hatch, this pattern is very successful.

Hooks: Up-eyed 12–14
Thread: Light brown (sherry spinner)
Tail: A few strands of ginger cock hackle
Body: Scarlet wool dubbed onto thread
Ribbing: Fine gold wire
Wings: Light grizzle hackle points
Hackle: Ginger cock
Head: Brown

1.
Take the thread down to the bend of the hook and tie in the ginger cock hackle which will be the tail. (As a matter of interest it is always much better to have the tail pointing down at a slight angle as it enhances the floating capability of the fly.) At the same point, tie in the fine gold wire.

2.
Dub the thread with the scarlet wool and wind down the shank (make sure that the wool is thinly wound) to the eye and tie in.

Lake Olive

3.
Select two nicely matched grizzle hackle points and place them together (front to front) and tie in. Separate the wings and make figure-of-eight turns to hold them in the semi-spent position.

4.
Wind on the ginger cock hackle and finish the fly in the usual way.

Light Cahill

An old favourite, originally tied by Daniel Cahill from New York State around 1880. He advocated the use of lemon Wood Duck feathers for the wings but they are not that plentiful and a satisfactory substitute are the flank feathers of the mallard drake. For some rivers, the Dark Cahill is probably a more suitable pattern, and so I have noted the different dressing on page 46. The Cahill is tied in the same way as the Light Hendrickson (*opposite*) and the step-by-step numbers below refer to the drawings that describe the tying of the Light Hendrickson.

Light Cahill

Hooks: Up-eyed 12–16
Thread: Yellow
Tail: Medium cream hackle fibres
Body: Cream seal fur
Hackle: Dark cream or ginger cock
Wings: Lemon Wood Duck (upright and divided) if available, otherwise mallard drake flank
Head: Yellow

1.
Select a bunch of lemon Wood Duck fibres and tie upright and divide.

2.
Take the yellow thread down to the bend of the hook and for the tail tie in a few medium cream hackle fibres. Spin some cream seal's fur onto the thread.

3.
Take the fur-laden thread back to just before the wing position.

4.
Wind on a ginger cock hackle and finish off the fly as usual.

Light Hendrickson

By substituting the appropriate materials the Dark Hendrickson, Light and Dark Cahills, and Light and Dark Adams are all tied in the same way. In fact, the wing is the same in all of these patterns.

Hooks: Up-eyed 12–14
Thread: Brown
Tail: Medium dun hackle
fibres
Body: Pinkish fox fur
Wings: Wood Duck flank
fibres
Hackle: Medium dun
Head: Brown

1.
Select a bunch of Wood Duck flank fibres. Tie upright and divide as in the drawing, using a figure-of-eight knot.

2.
Take the thread down to the bend and for the tail tie in a few medium dun hackle fibres. Spin some pinkish fox fur or poly dubbing onto the tying thread.

3.
Take the fur-laden thread back to just before the wing position.

4.
Wind on a medium dun hackle and finish off the fly.

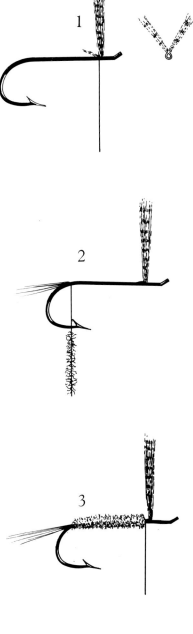

Lumme's Nalle Puh
(Lumme's Winnie-the-Pooh)

This is a caddis imitation more often than not fished in faster water. The colour varies from ginger to a very dark brown. A popular fly in Scandinavia for both trout and grayling.

Hooks: Up-eyed 8–14
Thread: Brown
Body: A mixture of ½ hot
orange seal's wool, ¼ yellow seal's wool, and ¼ light
brown fur from the hare's
ear and tied well round the
bend of the hook
Ribbing: Round gold tinsel
Hackle: Medium brown cock
hackle
Wing: Cinnamon bear fibres
or coarse poly yarn
Head: Clear varnish over hot
orange tying thread

Lumme's Nalle Puh

Lunn's Particular

W. J. Lunn tied this fly back in the 1930s. It is a pattern that belongs to Hampshire and is used extensively on the Test and the chalk streams of Buckinghamshire, Berkshire, and Wiltshire. It is most effective when the spinner of the Medium Olive is on the water.

Hooks: Up-eyed 14–16
Thread: Crimson
Tail: Fibres of natural red cock hackle
Body: Undyed Rhode Island Red hackle stalk
Wings: Medium blue dun hackle tips
Hackle: As for tail
Head: Crimson

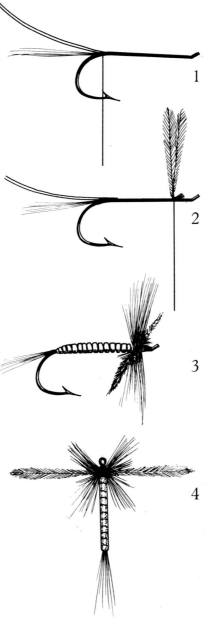

1.
Tie in a few fibres of natural red cock-hackle fibres for the tail. At the same point, tie in an undyed hackle quill from a Rhode Island Red hackle.

2.
Take the thread back up the hook and tie in two blue dun hackle tips. These are tied spent.

3.
Wind the hackle stalk up the shank to form the body and tie in a natural red cock hackle. Finish the fly in the usual way.

Mooi Moth

A South African pattern used extensively in the eastern part of the country. They do not have the numerous hatches that we are fortunate to have in the Northern Hemisphere and because of the heat the trout tend to lie deep. Nevertheless, on the occasion of a hatch this has proved a very popular pattern.

It is a point of interest to mention that although South Africa is approximately 6,000 miles (10,000 km) from London there is a great similarity in the flies used by both countries. I once asked R. Rosettenstein (a well-known fly-fisherman there) what his favourite dry-fly patterns were and he replied: Red Tag, Blue Dun, Black Gnat, March Brown, Ginger Quill, Coachman, Black Flying Ant, and the Mooi Moth!

Hooks: Up-eyed 12–14
Thread: Grey
Tail: Several fibres of medium blue dun cock hackle
Body: Well-marked peacock quill
Hackle: Medium blue dun cock
Wing: Grey mallard wing quill
Head: Grey

Olsen's Laerdal Fly

Pale Watery Dun

Olsen's Laerdal Fly

This fly is tied for sea trout in the fast Laerdal river in Norway.

It is an imitation of the caddis fly (*Phryganea grandis*) which dominates the insect life of many Norwegian rivers. Olsen's Laerdal Fly is often tied on a Wilson's dry-fly hook there, where the trout can weigh up to 20 pounds (9 kg).

Hooks: Up-eyed 6–12
Thread: Black

Tail: Three fibres from a pheasant-tail feather (cock)
Wing: Two bunches of badger hair, pointing forward with a 30° angle from the hook
Hackle: Covers ⅔ of the body from light brown to black
Head: Black

Olsen's Laerdal Fly

Pale Watery Dun

An excellent pattern from Freddie Rice. It is a very useful pattern when identification is difficult and the fly on the surface has a distant "watery" appearance.

It is not normally tied with wings but, if required, slips from the left and right starling primary feather may be used.

Hooks: Up-eyed 14–16
Thread: Light yellow
Tail: Four light blue dun or pale honey dun hackle fibres
Tag: Four turns of light yellow silk
Underbody: Light yellow silk
Body: Three herls from a light grey heron
Hackle: Pale olive or pale honey dun cock

3.

Take the tying thread to the bend of the hook (a hackle fibre tail can be tied on here if desired). Dub some black fur (natural or poly) onto the tying thread. Taking care not to trap the hackle fibres, wind the fur-laden thread back up the shank, using a dubbing needle to lift the hackle fibres away from the thread. Finish the fly in the usual way.

Parachute Black Gnat

William Brush of Detroit patented the parachute style in 1933. A parachute fly floats lightly down onto the water and presents a visible outline to the fish.

A vertical post of white calf's tail is tied in at mid-shank and is hackled around its base.

Hooks: Up-eyed 12–16
Thread: Black
Post: White calf's tail
Hackle: Black cock
Tail (optional): Black hackle fibre
Body: Black fur
Head: Black

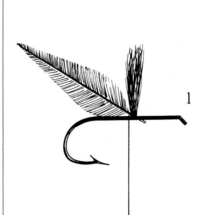

1.

At the point shown, tie in an upright bunch of white calf's tail. Apply varnish to the root and allow to dry (this gives a more solid base for the winding of the hackle). When dry, tie in a longish fibred black hackle.

2.

Wind this hackle around the base of the calf's tail and tie off.

Pheasant Tail

This dressing with the blue dun hackle and tail is A. Courtney Williams' recommendation for representing the Iron Blue. The fly can also be tied with honey dun cock.

Hooks: Down-eyed 12–16
Thread: Grey
Tail: Blue dun hackle fibres
Body: Cock-pheasant tail fibres
Ribbing: Gold wire
Hackle: Blue dun hackle fibres
Head: Grey

1.

Start the tying thread from just behind the eye and wind down the shank to the bend of the hook.

2.

Tie in the blue dun hackle fibres for the tail. At the same point, tie in a length of fine gold wire, and the cock-pheasant centre-tail fibres.

3.

Return the thread to the eye and varnish the shank, then wind on the pheasant tail over the wet shank to form the body, follow with the fine gold wire and tie off.

4.

Wind on the blue dun hackle and finish the fly in the usual way.

3.

Return the thread to where the wings are tied in. Follow this with the stripped herl. Tie in a medium dun hackle and wind in the usual way. Finish the fly with a small neat head.

All quill-bodied flies are tied this way. If they are hackled only, omit the wing procedure.

Quill Gordon

First tied by Theodore Gordon just before the turn of the century. He was not the most cooperative of men and consequently some of the original dressings are in doubt as he would not give any details.

He sometimes tied this fly with a fine gold wire rib. It has long been a favourite with American fishermen who, incidentally, also refer to it as the Gordon Quill.

Hooks: Up-eyed 12–16
Thread: Grey
Tail: Medium dun hackle fibres (blue-grey hackle fibre is sometimes preferred)
Body: Stripped peacock herl
Ribbing (optional): Fine gold wire
Wings: Wood Duck fibres (dyed mallard can be substituted)
Hackle: As tail
Head: Grey

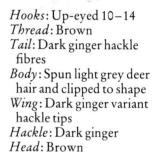

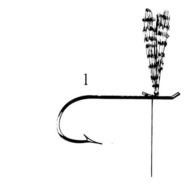

1.

Tie in a bunch of Wood Duck fibres (substitute: dyed mallard) and divide as in the drawings.

2.

Take the thread down to the bend of the hook and tie in a bunch of medium dun hackle fibres along with a stripped peacock herl.

Rat-Faced McDougal

Hooks: Up-eyed 10–14
Thread: Brown
Tail: Dark ginger hackle fibres
Body: Spun light grey deer hair and clipped to shape
Wing: Dark ginger variant hackle tips
Hackle: Dark ginger
Head: Brown

Red Ant

This is tied in the same way as the Black Ant (page 42).

Hooks: Up-eyed 14–16
Thread: Reddish brown
Body: Reddish-brown floss tied in two even humps
Wings: Grey hackle tips
Hackle: Reddish brown (natural)
Head: Brown

Red Quill

Closely associated with its lighter cousin the Ginger Quill. A firm favourite on the chalk streams and very much a pattern to have on any river. Attributed to Thomas Rushworth (1803) and a great favourite of the late F. M. Halford. There are various thoughts as to its imitative qualities but most would agree that it represents the Claret Dun. The pattern is tied like the Quill Gordon (*page 57*).

Hooks: Up-eyed 14–16
Thread: Brown
Tail: Red cock
Body: Peacock herl (stripped), taken from near the eye, giving light and dark edges
Hackle: Red goose cock
Head: Brown

Red Spinner

Hooks: Up-eyed 12–14
Thread: Brown
Tail: Light ginger cock-hackle fibres
Body: Red floss
Ribbing: Gold wire
Hackle: As tail
Head: Brown

1.
Take the brown tying thread down to the bend of the hook and tie in four light ginger cock-hackle fibres to form the tail. At the same place tie in a length of gold wire which will be the rib.

2.
Then tie in the red floss and wind down the shank to form the body and follow with the ribbing. Tie off. Select the hackle and tie in.

3.
Finish the fly in the usual way.

Rough Olive

A popular pattern in the south of England early in the season. It can be fished wet or dry. It is tied in the same way as the Grey Duster (*page 50*).

Hooks: Up-eyed 12–16
Thread: Olive
Tail: Blue dun cock-hackle fibres
Body: Olive seal's fur, ribbed gold wire
Hackle: Olive badger cock hackles
Head: Dark olive

Saabye's Fly

Tied by the famous Danish fly-dresser Svend Saabye for sea-trout fishing, it can vary in colour from a very light brown or grey to a very dark, almost black, colour.

Hooks: Up-eyed 10 long
  shank
Thread: Black
Tail: Short thick bunch of
  brown hackle fibres, pointing slightly downwards
Body: Tail half of hook only,
  light brown poly dubbing
Wing: Coarse poly yarn,
  brown
Hackle: Two long stiff saddle
  hackle feathers, one light
  grey and one light brown,
  mixed and wound both at
  the back and in front of the
  wings
Head: Black

Sherry Spinner

This is the spinner of the female Blue Winged Olive. Although its name would suggest its true colour, it does vary from the palest of ginger through to a deep red. The natural insect usually emerges in early summer and is most successful on broken water. This is the David Collyer dressing.

Hooks: Up-eyed 14
Thread: Pale orange

Tail: Light ginger cock-
  hackle fibres
Body: Deep orange floss and
  orange-dyed hackle stalk,
  unribbed
Ribbing: Gold wire
Wings: Pale blue dun hackle
  points set "spent"
Hackle: Rhode Island Red
  cock hackle

Sherry Spinner

Silver Sedge

Also known as the Grey Sedge and normally only found in the south of England, where it is specially effective on the chalk streams of Hampshire. A good pattern to tempt trout when they are smutting. This is F.M. Halford's pattern.

Hooks: Up-eyed 10–14
Thread: Tan
Body: White floss silk ribbed with fine flat silver tinsel
Body Hackle: Ginger cock
Wings: Grey duck
Hackle: Light ginger
Head: Tan

1.

At the bend, tie in a length of fine flat silver tinsel. This will form the rib. Take the tying thread back up the hook shank and tie in a length of white floss silk.

2.

Form the body of the fly by winding the floss down the hook-shank and back, then tie in a light ginger hackle.

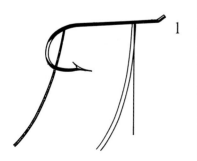

3.

Wind the hackle down the body and secure with the rib. Cut off the tip of the hackle.

4.

Select a slip of grey duck wing from a left and right feather and tie these on top of the hook. Finally, tie in another cock hackle in front of the wing.

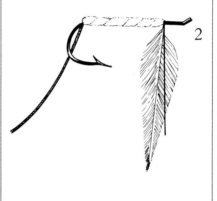

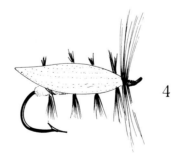

Sofa Pillow

This pattern is very popular in the United States. During the Stonefly hatches in the Rocky Mountains, the Sofa Pillow comes into its own, although there is little resemblance to the natural. The pattern is tied in brown or grey. I have illustrated the grey pattern.

Brown

Hooks: Down-eyed 4–12
Thread: Brown
Tail: Dyed crimson-red goose quill
Body: Red floss tied thin
Wing: Grey squirrel tied over body and extending to the end of tail
Hackle: Brown/natural red goose or game

Grey

As above but with yellow tail, yellow body, and grizzle hackle. The wing is grey squirrel.

1.

At the end of the hook, tie in a slip of red-dyed goose feather for the tail. At the same time tie in a length of flat, fine silver tinsel.

2.

Take the tying thread back up the shank and there tie in a length of red floss silk.

Treacle Parkin

This is a very popular fly in the north of England, where it is very often fished for grayling. It is a cousin of the Red Tag and identical in every way except for the orange tail.

The Red Tag was traced back to Martyn Flynn of Worcester who first tied the fly during the middle of the last century, when it was known as the Worcester Gem.

This pattern can also be fished wet with great effect and the only difference would be the substitution of red hen hackle for the red cock.

Hooks: Up-eyed 12–14
Thread: Brown or black
Tail: Orange wool
Body: Green/bronze peacock herl, preferably from below the eye
Hackle: Natural red cock hackle

1.

Tie in a tail of orange-coloured wool or silk. At the same point, tie in three or four strands of peacock herl.

2.

Wind the herl body by forming a rope with the peacock herl and tying thread. Tie off and cut away any surplus herl. At the same point, tie in a natural red cock hackle.

Wind on the hackle and complete the fly as fig. 3.

3.

For wet fly, use hen hackle, which is softer than cock hackle. Flies such as the Red Tag, Ke-he, Wormfly, and any other herl and hackle flies are all tied in the same way.

3.

Wind the floss up and down the shank to form the body, rib neatly with the silver tinsel, tie off, and remove the surplus. On top of the hook tie in a bunch of grey squirrel tail fibres. Finally, tie on a hackle of natural red game and finish in the usual way.

Tup's Indispensable

Very popular the world over, this pattern is the invention of a professional fly-dresser, R. S. Austin, around about the turn of the century. The Tups can be fished wet or dry (or as a nymph when it is tied to imitate a Pale Watery). The wet-fly version usually uses a blue dun hackle. I have included two dressings below, the original for interest and the modern tying for practical purposes.

Original

Hooks: Up-eyed 14–16
Thread: Yellow
Tail: Honey dun or bright-blue spade feather
Body: A mixture of tup's wool, cream-coloured seal's fur, lemon spaniel's fur, and a few pinches of mohair (this last ingredient was changed by the late G.E.M. Skues to crimson seal's fur)
Hackle: Light-blue hackle freckled thickly with gold
Head: Yellow

Modern

Hooks: Up-eyed 12–16 U.E.
Thread: Brown (sherry spinner)
Tail: Honey cock hackle
Body: Yellow floss silk with pink tup's wool or seal's fur at the front
Hackle: Honey cock hackle
Head: Brown

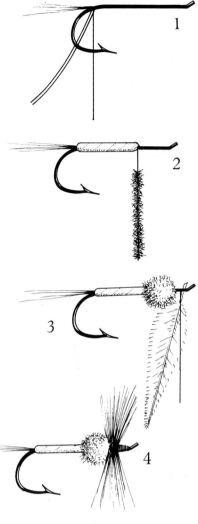

1.
Tie in a bunch of honey cock-hackle fibres and a length of yellow floss at the bend of the hook.

2.
Return tying thread up the hook and follow with the yellow body floss. Spin pink tup's wool or seal's fur dubbing onto the tying thread. This mixture gives an overall pinkish hue.

3.
Form the fur thorax and tie in a honey cock hackle.

4.
Wind on the hackle and finish off the fly in the usual way with a small neat head.

Verre Enn Minken
(Worse Than a Mink)

This is perhaps the most famous of the many good patterns tied by Erling Sand of Engerdal, a well-known professional flytier in Norway.

It is a very successful fly and is an imitation of the Yellow Mayfly (*Heptagenia sulphurea*) which is a very common insect in the Norwegian waters. Very popular for both trout and grayling.

Hooks: Down-eyed 10–14
Thread: Black
Tail: Three–five fibres from a pheasant-tail feather
Body: Lemon raffia
Ribbing: Pheasant-tail feather fibre
Hackle: Olive and brown cock feathers, mixed
Wing: Two cinnamon quill sections, pointing slightly backward
Head: Black

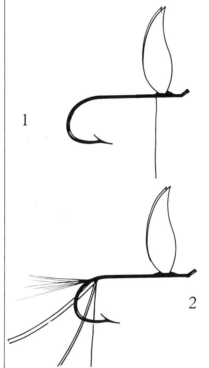

White Moth

One of the best patterns to use after dark. The fly does not imitate any particular natural. It has caught many sea trout and is really in its element towards the end of the summer.

Hooks: Up-eyed 10–12
Thread: White
Body: White wool
Ribbing: Silver wire
Hackle: White cock palmered along the body
Wings: White goose or swan quill

Wickham's Fancy

Hooks: Up-eyed 12–16
Thread: Yellow
Tail: Red cock-hackle fibres
Body: Flat gold tinsel
Ribbing: Fine gold wire
Hackle: Red or ginger game, palmered
Wings: Starling wing quill for the small hooks and grey goose wing quill for the large
Head: Yellow or black

1.

Select a matching pair of starling or grey duck quills from a left and a right wing. From each quill take a slip and place together. The natural out-curve of the feather aids the dry-fly wing. For the wet version, you would place the slips together with the natural curve inwards.

After winding on the tying thread in the usual way, tie the wing slips on top of the hook *(see page 11)*.

2.

Take the thread to the bend of the hook and tie in a bunch of natural light red cock-hackle fibres for the tail, a strip of flat gold tinsel, and a length of gold wire.

3.

Take the thread back up the hook. Follow with the flat gold tinsel. Tie off and get rid of the surplus tinsel. Tie in a light red cock hackle.

4.

Take the hackle, palmer-fashion, down the hook shank and secure with the ribbing wire. Remove the hackle point, after taking the ribbing wire down the body taking care not to trap in too many of the cock-hackle fibres. At this stage, tie in a further cock hackle of the same colour.

5.

Wind on the second hackle and form a neat head.

An angler playing out a fish that has been caught by dapping a Crane Fly (Daddy Long-Legs). Dapping requires a long rod, a floating line, and either a fly that imitates a natural or a heavily palmered, bushy fly tied on a long-shanked hook. The fly is made to dance, with the help of a strong breeze, on the surface of the water.

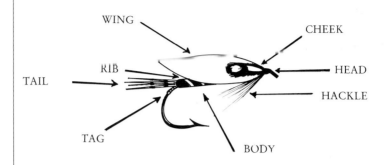

The wet-fly fisherman's aim is to fool the fish into believing that the submerged artificial that is being presented to it is its favourite food. The wet fly imitates a number of food possibilities for the hungry or curious fish: it can imitate a drowned surface fly or terrestrial (generally a spinner), an emerging nymph, an adult female that has swum to the bottom of the river or lake to deposit its eggs, or even a small fish (the red in the Parmachene Belle was intended by its designer to imitate a trout fin).

The wet fly is usually tied with a hen hackle, as this is softer than a cock hackle, and gives more life to the fly when it is submerged. Do not make the common mistake of over-dressing a wet fly (and indeed any fly). The wet fly, especially, should be tied sparsely. But it also has to sink. Now, this is not usually done by having an extra-heavy hook or ribbing material to weight the fly. It is the water-absorbing material that gives the wet fly its necessary weight, and this is yet another reason why hen hackles are used in preference to cock hackles.

The fly-fisherman often has two or three wet flies on the cast at the same time, as he works them through the water past the fish's lie. His one finger on the line is the only indicator he has to tell him that a fish has struck. Some fishermen are die-hard wet-fly men – just as others swear by the dry fly and scorn the wet. Both sectors have their own attractions, and why shouldn't the fisherman partake of both types of fishing, learning more about the fish and the flies in the process?

During a hatch, it is possible to see great activity near the surface, with the trout heading and tailing all over the place. It would be wrong to believe that the fish must be striking at surface flies. A closer look might show that their interest is in submerged flies that lie just beneath the surface.

Alder

Not everybody's favourite fly but nevertheless a pattern that has been with us for a long time. There are many anglers that swear by this fly for grayling. Charles Kingsley introduced this pattern in the latter part of the nineteenth century to imitate the natural fly, which is a terrestrial (or more properly, a semi-aquatic) fly. Kingsley's original dressing had a magenta-dyed peacock-herl body, but the pattern has gone through many variations since then and is now tied with an undyed peacock-herl body. In North America, it is sometimes tied with Golden Pheasant tippet fibres for a tail. Tie it in the same way as the March Brown (*page 82*).

Hooks: Down-eyed 10–14
Thread: Black
Body: Peacock herl
Wings: Dark speckled hen's wing
Hackle: Dyed black hen (tied under)
Head: Black

Alexandra

This fly was named after Princess Alexandra of Great Britain, but prior to that was universally known as the Lady of the Lake. It was originally tied by W. G. Turle and over the years became so effective and so successful that it was banned on some waters. I was privileged to be fishing in the Eastern Transvaal in Southern Africa some years ago when eleven fish, all 2 lbs (1 kg) + , were caught in three hours after five of us had fished all weekend trying every conceivable pattern with very little success.

It is basically a still-water pattern, probably more effective in cold water and usually fished on the point, well sunk and stripped in quite fast. It lost some of its popularity in recent years but there do seem to be signs of it returning. It is not the easiest of flies to tie as the peacock sword fibres and scarlet duck or goose wing are not the easiest of materials to manipulate.

Hooks: Down-eyed 8–12
Thread: Black
Tail: Scarlet duck or goose
Body: Flat silver tinsel
Ribbing: Oval silver tinsel
Hackle: Black cock (or hen)

Wing: Peacock sword herl and scarlet duck or goose
Head: Black

1.

Take the thread down to bend and tie in a strip of scarlet duck or goose for the tail. At the same point, tie in a length of oval silver tinsel.

2.

Return thread up the shank and tie in a strip of flat silver tinsel.

3.

Form the body by winding the tinsel down the hook and back followed by even turns of the rib. Tie off and remove surplus tinsel.

4.

Tie in a bunch of black cock or hen hackle fibres beneath the hook.

5.

Tie on a bunch of peacock sword fibres. When these have been tied in, flank them with a strip of scarlet duck or goose on either side. Complete the fly in the usual way. The Jungle Alexandra has a Jungle Cock feather flanking the wing instead of the red duck or goose.

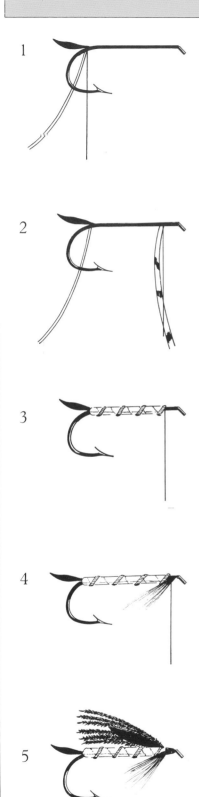

Black & Peacock Spider

This pattern was brought to public notice by Tom Ivens when he published his book "Stillwater Fly-Fishing" in 1952, though it has been traced back to 1816 when it was included by Bainbridge in his "Fly Dressers Guide".

It is probably one of the most effective still-water spider patterns ever used and can be fished in a variety of ways. In the early season, tied on a size 8 or 10, it is very effective when fished deep and slow. When the snails are floating, it should be fished in the surface film. The hook size should then be smaller (size 14) and a floating line and a greased leader to within 18″ (7 cm) of the fly should be used. In both cases, the longer the leader the more satisfactory the results.

This pattern is tied the same way as the Partridge & Orange (or any other spider pattern). The step-by-step numbers refer to the drawings on page 84.

Hooks: Down-eyed 8–14
Thread: Black
Body: Bronze peacock herl
Hackle: Large and soft black hen's hackle
Head: Black

1.
Tie in the bronze peacock herl at the bend of the hook.

2.
Wind the peacock herl up the shank, tie off and tie in the black hen hackle.

3.
Wind on the hackle and finish with a neat head and varnish.

Black Pennell

A pattern that was first tied by Cholmondeley-Pennell in the late nineteenth century. It is used extensively by the still and the running-water fisherman. In a size 8, it has a very impressive record as a sea-trout fly. It is normally tied on hook sizes 10–14, though Scotland will go down to 16s in wee-doubles for their loch fishing. Way up in the north of Scotland they sometimes prefer a hen hackle palmered along the body.

It is tied in the same way as William's Favourite, and the step-by-step numbers refer to the drawings on page 91.

Hooks: Down-eyed 10–14
Thread: Black
Tag: Fine silver tinsel
Tail: Golden pheasant tippet
Body: Thin black floss silk
Rib: Oval silver tinsel
Hackle: Long black cock—
    sparsely tied
Head: Black

1.
Take the thread down to the bend of the hook and tie in the golden pheasant tippet fibre feather to form the tail. At the same point, tie in the oval silver tinsel. Return the thread up the shank and tie in a length of black floss.

2.
Form the body by winding the floss down and back along the hook shank, following with the oval silver tinsel ribbing. Cut off the surplus.

3.
Wind on the black cock hackle and finish off the fly with a whip and varnish.

Black Spider

A pattern attributed to James Baillie. The author of *The Practical Angler*, published in 1857, W. C. Stewart, was without doubt the greatest fan of this pattern. He caught large amounts of trout in his lifetime but was rarely, if ever, found without the Black Spider in his team of flies. It must be tied very sparsely with a soft hackle.

> *Hooks*: Down-eyed 10–16
> *Thread*: Black
> *Body*: Black floss
> *Hackle*: Black hen
> *Head*: Black

1.

Tie in a length of black floss at the bend of the hook.

2.

Take the thread back to the eye, form the body with the black floss, and tie off. Tie in a soft black hen hackle (some prefer to tie it in by the tip).

3.

Wind on the hackle and finish the fly in the usual way.

4.

Some anglers prefer a fly with a much shorter body.

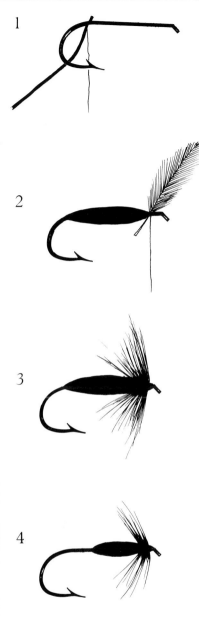

Blae & Black

A traditional pattern certainly in use at the turn of the century and very popular in Ireland as a sea-trout fly. I am unable to trace its origin but it has been referred to as the duck fly in Wales. Very effective fished on the top dropper "loch style" during the early part of the season. It is tied in the same way as the Mallard & Claret and the step-by-step numbers refer to drawings on page 81.

> *Hooks*: Down-eyed 10–14
> *Thread*: Black
> *Tail*: Golden Pheasant tippets
> *Body*: Black wool
> *Ribbing*: Oval silver tinsel
> *Hackle*: Black hen
> *Wings*: Starling wing
> *Head*: Black

1.

At the bend, tie in a few fibres of Golden Pheasant tippet feathers to form the tail of the fly. At the same point, tie in a length of oval silver tinsel, which is the ribbing. Dub the tying thread with black wool.

2.

Wind the dubbed thread down the hook shank. Follow with the ribbing.

3.

At the point shown, tie in a false hackle of black hen. Select two strips of starling wing from a left and right feather, place them together, and tie onto the top of the hook.

4.

Complete the fly with a neat head and varnish.

When the Blae & Black is tied for brown trout, in the smaller sizes, the black hen hackle is often replaced by a black cock hackle, as this is easier to tie small.

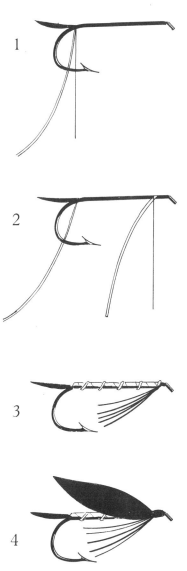

Butcher
Bloody Butcher
Kingfisher Butcher

This pattern was first tied in the early nineteenth century by two anglers from Tunbridge Wells, a butcher called Moon and his friend Jewhurst. Originally known as Moon's Fly, it became known in its present name in about 1836. These two fellow anglers tied the pattern to represent their trade with the red tail being the meat and the blue wing the traditional apron.

It is an excellent fly, known worldwide, and has saved many a blank day. In the early part of the season when the water is cold, it produces many trout from the deep water. It is a very popular fly in Scotland and is often fished as part of a team of flies anywhere from the point to the top dropper.

It has also a part to play in sea-trout fishing, in a size 8, but as many of the sea-trout flies have a black/silver combination, this is not too surprising.

Its two variants are the Bloody Butcher, which has a scarlet hackle instead of black, and the Kingfisher Butcher, which has a blue tail, gold body, and orange hackle.

Hooks: Down-eyed 10–16; 8 for sea trout
Thread: Black
Tail: Red ibis or substitute
Body: Flat silver tinsel
Ribbing: Oval silver tinsel
Hackle: Black cock or hen's hackle
Wings: From the blue-black section of a feather from a mallard wing
Head: Black

1.
Take the thread down the shank to the bend and tie in the red ibis substitute for the tail. Tie in a length of oval silver tinsel.

2.
Take the thread back down the shank and tie in a length of flat silver tinsel. Form the body by wrapping the hook shank with the flat tinsel down to the bend and back. Rib this with the oval tinsel. Cut away any surplus tinsel. Tie in a bunch of black hackle fibres beneath the hook.

3.
On top of the hook, tie two slips of blue mallard (left and right feathers). Finish the fly with a whip finish in the usual way.

Bloody Butcher

Coachman

A traditional fly dating back to the early 1800s. It can be fished wet or dry. The fly is tied in the same way as the March Brown (*page 82*). It is found all over the world and has a variant—the Royal Coachman, which made its name in North America. Another variant, the Leadwing Coachman, has the same pattern except for the wings, which are mallard wing-quill segments.

> *Hooks*: Down-eyed 10–14
>   for wet; up-eyed 14 for dry
> *Thread*: Brown or black
> *Body*: Peacock herl from the
>   stem
> *Hackle*: Red or ginger cock
> *Wings*: Duck primary quill
>   white
> *Head*: Brown or black

Cinnamon & Gold

A good sea-trout pattern and fished to its best advantage in the middle of the summer. It is tied in the same way as the Butcher, and the step-by-step figures refer to drawings for the Butcher (*opposite*). In some areas, they omit the tail.

> *Hooks*: Down-eyed 8–14
> *Thread*: Brown or black
> *Tail* (optional): Golden
>   Pheasant tippet fibres
> *Body*: Flat gold
> *Ribbing*: Oval gold tinsel
> *Hackle*: Cinnamon-coloured
>   cock hackle
> *Wing*: Cinnamon hen wing
>   feather
> *Head*: Brown or black

3.

Form the body by wrapping the hook shank with the tinsel down to the bend and back. Rib with the oval gold tinsel. Cut away surplus tinsel and beneath the hook tie in a bunch of cinnamon-coloured cock-hackle fibres.

4.

On the top of the hook tie two slips of cinnamon-coloured hen wing feather. Whip and varnish to finish.

1.

Take the thread down the shank and tie in the Golden Pheasant tippet fibre feather to form the tail. At the same point, tie in a length of oval gold tinsel.

2.

Take the thread back down the shank and tie in a length of flat gold tinsel.

Cinnamon & Gold (variant)

Royal Coachman

Connemara Black

This fly originated in the west of Ireland and has been responsible for killing many trout and grayling. It has also become one of the more successful sea-trout patterns fished just below the surface. It is excellent for late evening fishing in warm weather.

Its black-silver combination is often found in the more popular sea-trout flies.

Hooks: Down-eyed 10–14;
  8 for sea trout
Thread: Black
Tail: Golden Pheasant crest
Body: Black seal's fur or black
  wool
Ribbing: Fine oval silver
  tinsel
Hackle: Black cock with Blue
  Jay outside
Wing: Bronze mallard
Head: Black

1.
Take the thread down the hook and tie in the Golden Pheasant crest to form the tail. At the same point, tie in the oval silver tinsel, dub on the black seal's fur and wind down the shank to form the body.

2.
Follow with the tinsel to form the ribbing.

3.
Tie in the black cock hackle (under the hook) and also tie in some Blue Jay hackle on the outside of the black cock hackle.

4.
Tie in the wing of bronze mallard on top of the hook, whip and varnish in the usual way.

Cowdung

This pattern can be fished wet or dry. The natural is a land-bred fly that gets blown onto the water and the result is a vigorous rise by the trout. There has always been a school that thinks that the land-bred patterns are not worth their place in the fly box, but this one, together with the Alder and Daddy Long Legs (Crane Fly), has killed many fish. The pattern given here is by the nineteenth-century fly-fisherman Alfred Ronalds. It is tied in the same way as the March Brown (*page 82*).

Hooks: Down-eyed 12–14
Thread: Brown
Body: Chenille, dyed olive
Ribbing: Light-green silk
Hackle: Honey dun—
  darkish
Wings: Dark honey dun
  hackle tips
Head: Brown

Dai Ben

A classic fly from Mid/South Wales. Fished extensively on such rivers as the Teifi. The original hackle came from the rare Andalusian Blue Cock and many fishermen in South Wales bred their own birds solely to obtain their blue dun feathers. It is tied in the same way as the Black Spider (*page 69*).

Hooks: Down-eyed 10–14
Thread: Brown
Body: Rabbit or hare's fur
Ribbing: Gold tinsel
Hackle: Blue dun cock
Head: Brown

Dunkeld

Dunkeld

The pattern is a very old one, and there is very little information as to its origin. It almost certainly started life as a salmon fly, and, over the years, it has been modified to suit the still-water and lake anglers who have varying ideas as to its best position in a team and what conditions suit it the best. It has caught fish on the bob, dropper, and the point. It can be fished fast or slow, deep or shallow. I have found it a more successful fly at the latter end of the season. It appears for sale these days generally without the Jungle Cock eye, which was barred from being imported due to conservation reasons.

Hooks: Down-eyed 10–14;
  8 for sea trout
Thread: Brown
Tail: Golden Pheasant crest
  feather
Body: Flat gold tinsel
Ribbing: Gold wire or oval
  gold tinsel
Hackle: Palmered hot orange
Wings: Bronze mallard
Cheeks (optional): Jungle
  Cock
Head: Brown (or black)

1.

Take thread to bend of the hook and tie in a Golden Pheasant crest feather for the tail. Tie in also a length of fine oval gold tinsel. Take the thread back down the shank and tie in a strip of flat gold tinsel.

2.

Form the body by taking the flat gold tinsel down to the bend of the hook and back again, tie off, and cut away the surplus. Tie in a hot orange hackle.

3.

Wind the hackle, palmer-style, down the hook and secure with the ribbing tinsel. Wind the ribbing tinsel up the hook shank, taking care not to trap too many hackle fibres in the process. Secure ribbing tinsel and cut off the hackle point at the rear.

4.

Select four slips of bronze mallard (two left and two right) and tie on top of the hook. It was usual to tie two Jungle Cock feathers on either side of the wing but, nowadays, these are dispensed with.

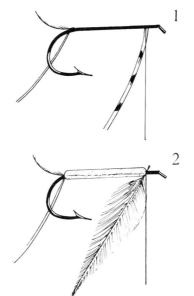

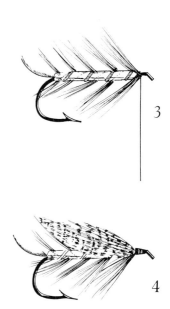

Gold-ribbed Hare's Ear (British)

February Red

A very old pattern from the English North Country, the February Red was tied to imitate one of the early-season Stoneflies.

Hooks: Down-eyed 14
Thread: Claret
Body: Orange mohair or
   seal's fur
Hackle: Blue dun hen of a
   smoky tint
Head: Claret

Gold-ribbed Hare's Ear

Hare's ear as a material has become one of the most popular materials of all time. It is made into a dry fly, a nymph (long and short shank) and a wet fly (with and without wings). The wet fly without a wing looks like a nymph, but I have photographed the two for identification purposes. The materials are the same in all cases. Tie in the same way as the Gold-ribbed Hare's Ear nymph (*page 24*).

Hooks: Down-eyed 10–14
   short shank
Thread: Brown
Tail: Hare's fur
Body: Hare's fur
Ribbing: Oval gold tinsel
Wings: Starling
Head: Brown

Green Peter

One of the traditional Irish Sedge or Caddis patterns and a firm favourite on the limestone lakes of the Emerald Isle. In recent years, it has received a certain degree of popularity on the lakes of Wales and the major reservoirs of England. An excellent pattern during a hatch of Sedge.

Hooks: Down-eyed 12–14
Thread: Olive or black
Body: Light-green seal's fur
Wing: Bronze mallard
Ribbing: Fine gold tinsel
Hackle: Light natural-red
   cock-hackle fibres
Head: Olive

1.

At the bend, tie in a strand of gold tinsel. Dub the tying thread with some light-green seal's fur or substitute.

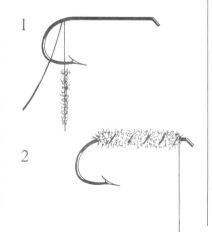

2.

Take the fur-laden thread down the shank. Follow with the ribbing.

3.

The next stage is the hackle; tie in a bunch of light natural-red hackle fibres.

4.

Select suitable strips of bronze mallard (two from a left, two from a right). Place on top of the hook and tie in. Form the head and finish in the usual way.

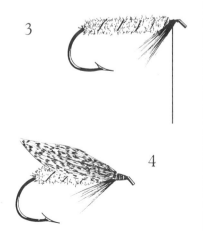

Greenwell's Glory

Another internationally well-known fly which originated on the Tweed in the 1850s. Canon William Greenwell asked a local professional flytier named James Wright to produce an artificial fly from a live Olive Dun which the Canon had captured by the water. The result was successful—the records which have been written all over the world speak for themselves. It was basically a wet fly and only later did it make its mark as a dry pattern.

As with all the other traditional patterns, there is a certain amount of controversy as to the origin of the various patterns, and this one is no exception. A man called Aitkin could lay claim to this pattern, having a pattern very similar a few years before the Canon.

> *Hooks*: Down-eyed 12–14
> *Thread*: Yellow or primrose
> *Body*: Yellow or primrose
>   silk, waxed with cobblers'
>   wax
> *Ribbing*: Fine gold wire
> *Hackle*: Furnace hen, chest-
>   nut with black centre, or
>   Coch-y-Bondhu cock
> *Wings*: Dark starling primary
> *Head*: Primrose

1.

At the bend of the hook, tie in a length of gold wire.

2.

Form the body with the primrose tying silk (a heavier body can be tied using floss, if so desired). Rib with gold wire.

3.

The next stage is the hackle. Tie in either a few fibres of light furnace hen beneath the hook as a false hackle or wind on a complete hackle in the usual way, taking a few turns of thread over the hackle to force it below the hook.

4.

Select from a right and left feather slips of dark starling and tie on top of the hook. Finish fly in the usual way.

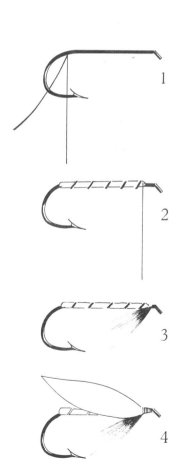

Grenadier

Originated in Somerset and first tied by Dr. Bell of Wrington who fished for most of his life at Blagdon. A very easy fly to tie.

Hooks: Down-eyed 12–14
Thread: Brown or black
Body: Hot orange seal's fur or
floss
Ribbing: Oval gold tinsel
(some prefer embossed)
Hackle: Light furnace hackle
(very sparse)
Head: Brown or black

1.

Take the tying thread down the hook to the bend and tie in a length of oval gold tinsel. At the same place, tie in a length of hot orange floss (some prefer seal's fur, in which case it helps to wax the thread first).

2.

Return the thread to the eye and wind the floss onto the shank, thus making the body. Follow with the ribbing and tie off.

3.

Select your hackle, which needs to be sparse when tied; tie in, and finish in the usual way.

Grouse Series

Originating in the north of England, these patterns are much sought after for sea trout. The grouse wing and dark hackle remain throughout the range, but the body can be green, orange, red, yellow, or claret. The step-by-step numbers refer to the drawings for the Mallard & Claret (*page 81*).

Hooks: Down-eyed 8–14
Thread: Brown
Tail: Golden Pheasant tippet
Body: Wool or seal's fur
Ribbing: Oval silver or gold
tinsel
Hackle: Usually dark natu-
ral-red game (some have
a preference for medium)
Wings: Wing feathers of
grouse
Head: Black

1.

At the bend, tie in a few fibres of Golden Pheasant tippet feather to form the tail. At the same point, tie in a length of tinsel. Dub the claret wool or seal's fur onto the thread.

Grouse & Claret

2.

Wind the dubbed thread down the shank to form the body. Follow with the ribbing.

3.

At the point shown, tie in a false hackle of dark natural-red game hackle fibres.

4.

Select four strips of grouse wing feather from a left and a right feather, place them together and tie them on top of the hook. Complete the fly in the usual manner with a varnished head.

Hawthorn

The natural Hawthorn is jet black and about ½ inch (1.3 cm) long. It has been written about for centuries, Dame Juliana Berners being the first to record it (1486). Izaak Walton also mentions it in *The Compleat Angler*. The pattern can be fished wet or dry, and it is best on lake and river water when the naturals are active.

> *Hooks*: Down-eyed 12–14
> *Thread*: Black
> *Body*: Black ostrich herl
> *Legs* (optional): Stripped
>   ostrich herl
> *Hackle*: Black cock
> *Wings*: Palest starling wing
>   feather
> *Head*: Black

1.

At the bend, tie in the black ostrich herl. Wind up the shank to form the body, and tie off. If you opt to have legs, tie the stripped ostrich herl in on either side of the hook, pointing backwards.

2.

Tie in the black cock hackle. Place the selected left and right palest starling wing feathers together and tie on top of the hook.

3.

Complete in the usual way by whipping and varnishing.

Heckham Peckham

An excellent pattern for lake fishing and for sea trout. Very popular in North America, it was first tied by William Murdock of Aberdeen. There are two main variants, the Heckham and Black, and the Heckham and Silver. It is tied in the same way as the Mallard & Claret and the step-by-step description corresponds to the drawings on page 81.

> *Hooks*: Down-eyed 10–14
>   (8's for sea trout)
> *Thread*: Black
> *Tail*: Three or four fibres of
>   Golden Pheasant tippet
> *Body*: Red seal's fur
> *Ribbing*: Silver tinsel
> *Hackle*: Red cock
> *Wings*: White-tipped mallard
>   feather (with a green sheen)
> *Head*: Black

1.

Take the thread down the shank to the bend and tie in the fibres of Golden Pheasant tippet feather to form the tail of the fly. At the same point, tie in a length of silver tinsel for the ribbing. Dub the seal's fur onto the thread.

2.

Wind the dubbed thread down the shank. Follow with the ribbing.

3.

At the point shown in the drawing (*page 81*), tie in a false hackle of red cock-hackle fibres.

4.

Select the white-tipped mallard feather for the wing and tie in on top of the hook. Finish with a whip and varnish.

Invicta Silver

Hofland's Fancy

A pattern first tied in the 1830s by T.C. Hofland to imitate a small Spinner that he kept seeing on the water. It is still a popular fly especially in the high summer and can be fished wet or dry.

> *Hooks*: Down-eyed 12–14
> *Thread*: Dark brown
> *Tail*: Two or three strands of red cock hackle
> *Body*: Reddish dark-brown floss
> *Hackle*: Red cock hackle
> *Wings*: Woodcock wing
> *Head*: Dark brown

1.

Take the thread down to the bend of the hook and tie in three strands of red cock hackle to form the tail. At the same point, tie in the floss and wind down the shank to form the body.

2.

Tie in the hackle.

3.

Select the woodcock wing from left and right feathers and tie on top of the hook.

4.

Whip and varnish.

Invicta

James Ogden of Cheltenham, who was a master of his trade, tied this pattern in the late nineteenth century to imitate the hatching Sedge pupa. It is probably the best known of all Sedge patterns and has been responsible for killing large amounts of fish all over the world. In many places, especially in Norway, it is regarded as an excellent sea-trout fly. In the early summer, when the Sedges are beginning to hatch, the fly comes into its own. It is a fly that needs to be fished either in the surface film or just under it.

> *Hooks*: Down-eyed 8–14
> *Thread*: Olive
> *Tail*: Golden Pheasant crest
> *Body*: Yellow-dyed seal's fur (or yellow wool)
> *Ribbing*: Oval gold tinsel
> *Hackle*: Light-red cock hackle palmered from shoulder to tail
> *Throat*: Blue Jay or dyed Guinea-fowl
> *Wing*: Hen-pheasant centre-tail
> *Head*: Olive

1.

At the bend, tie in a Golden Pheasant crest feather. At the same point, tie in a length of tinsel for the rib. Dub some yellow seal's fur onto the tying thread.

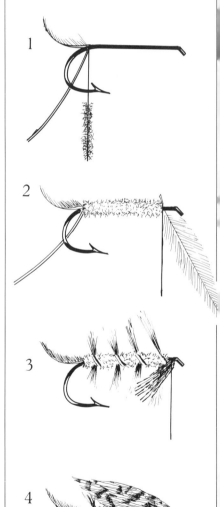

Red-tailed Invicta

2.
Take the fur-laden thread down the hook shank and tie in a light-red cock hackle.

3.
Wind the cock hackle, palmer-style, down to the bend of the hook and secure with the ribbing tinsel, winding the tinsel down the body. Tie off, remove any surplus hackle fibre and tinsel, and tie in a false hackle of Blue Jay fibres.

4.
Select a slip of feather from either side of a hen-pheasant centre-tail and tie in on top of the hook. Finish the fly in usual way.

John Storey

The Storey family have lived by the River Rye in Yorkshire since the early 1850s. The Ryedale Anglers Club employed John Storey as a river keeper when he was twenty-three and for the next fifty-seven years the river became his life. The original pattern has changed somewhat from a wet fly to a dry one and John Storey's grandson Arthur experimented with the winging of the fly. Finding that the then popular upright winging was difficult for many fly-dressers, he allowed the winging to lean forward over the eye. It turned out to be even more successful than the original. When I approached Arthur Storey for the dressing he pointed out that he is tying a variant for grayling with a ginger hackle.

> *Hooks*: Down-eyed 14–16
> *Thread*: Black
> *Body*: Peacock herl
> *Wing*: Small whole crest feather from an adult mallard (the feathers of the immature birds are *not* suitable because of their brownish tinge).
> *Hackle*: Rhode Island Red cock hackle
> *Head*: Black

Ke-He

A very popular pattern in Scotland. It was conceived by two anglers in 1932, Messrs Kemp and Heddle who used to visit Loch Harray in the Orkneys regularly. They tied this fly to imitate the countless numbers of bees that are blown onto the lake. It has changed from its original dressing slightly as it used to have a red cock hackle and no red tag under the tippets.

> *Hooks*: Down-eyed 10–12
> *Thread*: Black
> *Tail*: Golden Pheasant tippets with red tag under
> *Body*: Bronze peacock herl
> *Hackle*: Rhode Island Black (some prefer Red)
> *Head*: Black

1.
At the bend, tie in a few fibres of Golden Pheasant tippet feathers with a red wool tag under. At the same point, tie in the bronze peacock herl.

2.
Wind the herl up the shank to the eye, leaving room for the Rhode Island Black hackle which is then tied in.

3.
Finish with a neat head and varnish.

Machadodorp

A very popular South African fly named after the town in the Eastern Transvaal.

Hooks: 6–12
Thread: Black
Tail: Iron blue cock
Body: Grey chenille
Hackle: Iron blue cock
Wing: Grey duck
Head: Black

1.
Take the thread down the shank to the bend in the hook and tie in a few strands of iron blue cock hackle to form the tail.

2.
At the same point, tie in the grey chenille and wind down the shank to form the body.

3.
Tie in the hackle, select the grey duck wing from left and right feathers and tie on top of the hook.

4.
Whip and varnish.

Mallard Series

Another fly that has a worldwide reputation. Its origin is not that definite, although most people would agree that William Murdoch, a well-known Aberdeen flytier who has also had his name linked with the Heckham Peckham, was the person responsible for the fly in its present form. There are various records, dating back to 1840, that show that a very similar dressing was used for loch type fishing but without the golden pheasant tippet feathers.

It is a fly that can be used throughout the season very successfully, but it should be pointed out that, whereas wool can be used on a lot of patterns as a substitute, this is one fly that should have the dyed seal's fur for its sparkle.

Mallard & Claret

Hooks: Down-eyed 10–14;
  for sea trout, use an 8
Thread: Black
Tail: Golden Pheasant tippets
Body: Claret seal's fur
Ribbing: Oval gold tinsel
Hackle: Dark claret (or light
  red or black)
Wing: Bronze mallard
Head: Black

All flies in the Mallard series can be tied this way, i.e., Mallard & Blue, Mallard & Yellow, Mallard & Red, etc., etc. The only difference is that the seal's fur body is dyed the appropriate colour.

1.

At the bend of the hook, tie in a few fibres of Golden Pheasant tippet feather to form the tail of the fly. At the same point, tie in a length of gold oval tinsel. This is the rib. Dub claret seal's fur onto the tying thread.

2.

Wind the dubbed thread down the hook shank. Follow with the rib.

3.

At the point shown, tie a false hackle of claret cock-hackle fibres.

4.

Select four strips of brown mallard shoulder feathers from a left and right feather, place them together and tie them on top of the hook; complete the fly with a neat head.

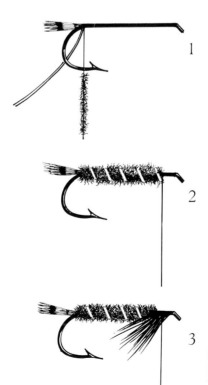

March Brown

A fly that has been with us since the seventeenth century. In the wet version it is normally winged and can be used on river or lake. The hackled version is used for upstream river fishing. It is excellent in broken water and will be found in most flyboxes. It is an early-season fly, more common in the Welsh valleys and the north of England than in the south.

Hooks: Down-eyed for wet
   10 −14; up-eyed for dry
   12 −14
Thread: Brown
Tail: Fibres from brown
   speckled partridge hackle
Body: Fur from hare's body
Ribbing: Gold wire
Hackle: Same as tail
Wings: Hen pheasant, paired
   left and right primary wing
   feather
Head: Brown (or black)

Gold March Brown

2.

Take the tying thread and dubbing up the shank, forming the body of the fly. Follow this with even turns of the gold rib.

3.

Form a hackle with brown partridge feather.

4.

Select matching left and right slips of hen-pheasant wing quill and tie on top of the hook. Finish as usual.

Silver March Brown

The two variants, shown centre and above, are the same as the March Brown, except that their bodies are of flat tinsel ribbed with oval tinsel (gold or silver, depending on the variant required).

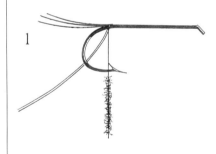

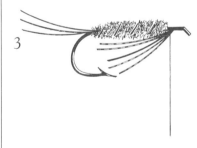

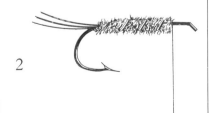

1.

Select a bunch of brown partridge hackle fibres for the tail and tie them in at the bend. At the same point, tie in a length of gold wire. Dub some hare's fur for the body onto the tying thread.

Parmachene Belle

This fly is named after the Parmachene Lake and was first tied by Henry P. Wells in the late 1800s. A very popular fly in North America. It is not so popular in Great Britain, but tied on a size-8 hook it has caught many sea trout in Devon. In Scandinavia, it is often used for brook trout. It is sometimes fished dry in a very small size.

> *Hooks*: Down-eyed 10–14
> *Thread*: Black
> *Tail*: Married strands of red and white goose
> *Butt* (optional): Black ostrich herl
> *Body*: Lemon-yellow floss or wool
> *Ribbing*: Gold tinsel
> *Hackle*: Mixed white and red
> *Wing*: Married strands of red and white goose or duck
> *Head*: Black

This fly has what is termed as a built wing. The individual fibre of every feather is joined to its neighbour by a series of minute hooks (one could almost say a 'Velcro' system). This natural linking can be used to join feathers of different colours to build a composite wing.

1.

Prepare the wings first. Select a right-side white goose or duck quill and a red-dyed similar feather. From the white feather, cut off two slim slips. From the red feather, cut off one slim slip. Hold the tips of these slips gently between thumb and finger and with the thumb and finger of the other hand stroke the feathers together. You will find that they will naturally adhere to one another. Now repeat this operation with a left-side feather and you have the wings ready.

2.

The whole operation can be repeated with narrower slips to form the tail of the fly. However, some patterns

Parmachene Belle

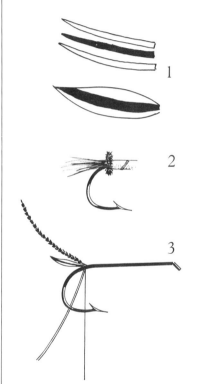

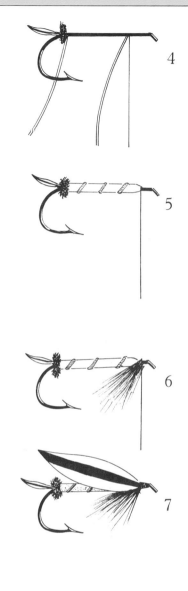

dispense with the built tail and use a bunch of red and white hackle fibres for the tail, as shown here.

3.

Take the tying thread down to the bend of the hook and tie in the married slips of goose or the hackle fibres for the tail. At the same point, tie in a length of gold tinsel and some black ostrich herl.

4.

Form a butt with the ostrich herl. Take the thread back down the hook and tie in a length of yellow floss.

5.

Form the body by winding the floss down the hook shank and back. Follow this with the rib. Cut away surplus.

6.

Next stage is the hackle. Stroke the dyed red and white hackle fibres below the hook, tie off, and remove the surplus feather.

7.

Now pick up the wing slips and tie in on top of the hook. Finish the fly with a whip finish in the usual way.

Partridge Series

To exemplify this series, we have chosen the Partridge & Orange, which is a spider pattern representing the February Red and other Stoneflies. It fishes well in faster, broken waters. You will probably find it fished upstream for grayling as well as trout. When the orange silk is wet, it turns the beautiful mahogany colour of the natural. It is a pattern that should not be forgotten on still waters and is generally fished on a size-14 hook late on in the day.

Variants are Partridge & Red, & Yellow, & Green, & Claret. That is, to say, the body has the differing colour.

Partridge & Orange

Hooks: Down-eyed 14
Thread: Hot orange
Body: Bright orange floss or silk
Hackle: Brown partridge back feather
Head: Orange

1.

Tie in orange floss at the bend of the hook.

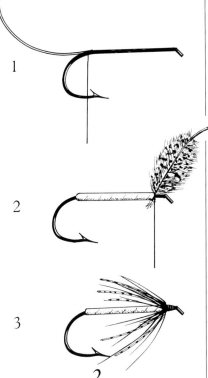

2.

Wind the floss up the shank, tie off, cut off surplus body material, and tie in a brown partridge hackle by the tip.

3.

Wind on the hackle and finish with a whip finish and a dab of clear varnish.

Pennell's Claret

Hooks: Down-eyed 10–14
Thread: Black (or claret)
Tail: Golden Pheasant crest and tippet
Body: Claret seal's fur
Ribbing: Gold tinsel (some prefer oval gold tinsel)
Hackle: Furnace cock
Head: Black (or claret)

1.

Take the thread down to the bend in the hook and tie in the golden pheasant tippet fibres with a golden pheasant crest on top.

2.

At the same point, tie in the gold tinsel.

3.

Dub the claret seal's fur onto the thread, and wind down the hook shank, forming the body.

4.

Follow with the gold tinsel, making even turns.

5.

Tie in the furnace cock hackle and shape it over the body.

Peter Ross

One of the most popular flies ever tied. Probably found in everybody's fly-box at some time or another. It was the brainchild of Peter Ross, a shopkeeper in Killin, Scotland, who was not quite satisfied with the popular fly of that era, the Teal & Red. He was not a flytier so he asked a local man to tie a few flies to his specifications. The results are now history and not only has it become one of the great reservoir flies of all time, it accounts for more than its fair share of sea trout. It is tied in the same way as the Teal & Red (*page 88*), except for the body, which is in two parts in the Peter Ross.

Hooks: Down-eyed 10–14;
    8 for sea trout
Thread: Black
Tail: Golden Pheasant tippets
Body: Front 1/3 scarlet seal
    fur, rear 2/3 flat silver tinsel
Ribbing: Fine oval tinsel
Hackle: Black hen or cock
Wing: Barred teal
Head: Black

Professor

Named after Professor John Wilson who was appointed Professor of Philosophy at Edinburgh University in 1820. An excellent pattern for sea trout and very popular all over the world. It is usually fished wet but can be tied dry.

Hooks: Down-eyed 8–12
Thread: Brown
Tail: Two or three long fibres
    of red ibis feather
Body: Primrose yellow
Ribbing: Oval gold tinsel
Hackle: Ginger cock
Wings: Mottled grey mallard
Head: Yellow

1.
Take the brown thread down the shank to the bend in the hook and tie in the long fibres of the red ibis feather (or substitute) to form the tail. At the same point, tie in the oval gold tinsel and the yellow floss.

2.
Wind the floss down the hook shank to form the body and follow with the ribbing of oval gold tinsel.

3.
Tie in the ginger cock hackle and then the wing, which is tied on top of the hook.

4.
Finish off in the usual way.

Queen of the Water

Another very popular fly from North America. Fished mainly in the eastern United States. It can be fished wet or dry and is often found as the top dropper on a team of flies. It is tied in the same way as Wickham's Fancy (*page 63*).

Hooks: Down-eyed 10–14
Thread: Brown or black
Body: Orange floss
Hackle: Brown, palmer tied
    along the body
Wing: Teal or grey mallard
Head: Brown or black

Red Tag

This fly was a pattern tied by Martyn Flynn in the middle of the last century in Worcestershire. He called it the Worcester Gem and used it extensively on the Lugg, Arrow, and Teme. An excellent fly for trout and grayling. Tied with a yellow or orange tail, it becomes the Treacle Parkin. It can be fished wet or dry.

Hooks: Down-eyed for wet
  and up-eyed for dry: 12–16
Thread: Brown
Tail: Red floss or wool
Body: Bronze/green peacock
  herl from the peacock eye
  feather
Hackle: Natural or bright-
  red game hen for wet fly
  (cock for dry)
Head: Brown (or black)

1.

Take the tying thread down the shank to the bend and tie in the red tail. At the same point, tie in the peacock herl, and wind it down the shank to form the body.

2.

Stop just before the eye to allow the red game hackle to be tied in.

3.

Whip and varnish in the usual way.

Snipe & Purple

A very popular pattern from the North of England, where it is generally accepted as imitating the Iron Blue Dun. A spider pattern that relies on the hackle being worked by the current. It is essential to tie very sparsely. The hackle should be as dark as possible.

Hooks: Down-eyed 12–16
Thread: Purple
Body: Purple floss silk
Hackle: The dark hackle
  found close to the centre
  elbow joint of the snipe's
  wing
Head: Purple

1.

Take the thread down the shank to the bend and tie in the purple floss silk.

2.

Wind the floss back up the shank to form the body making sure that the floss is only finely covering the shank.

3.

Tie in the hackle, whip, and varnish.

Soldier Palmer

A very old pattern dating back many centuries. Palmer was used as a word to describe the returning pilgrims from the Holy Land, bringing palms. It can be fished wet or dry. It has been thought for some time that this pattern represented a type of caterpillar. The American Wooly Worm is a recent adaptation of this pattern.

Hooks: Down-eyed 10–16;
  up-eyed for dry
Thread: Scarlet or black
Body: Scarlet wool
Ribbing: Very fine oval gold
  tinsel
Hackle: Natural red game
  (cock)
Head: Black

1.

At the bend of the hook, tie in a

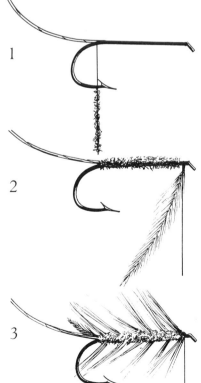

length of oval gold tinsel, dub onto the thread some red seal's fur (wool can be used as alternative).

2.

Take the fur-laden thread back up the body and tie in a natural red cock hackle.

3.

Palmer the hackle down the body, secure with the ribbing tinsel, take the tinsel down the shank.

4.

Cut off the surplus tinsel and remove the hackle point at the rear. Finish the fly as usual.

Teal Blue & Silver

Teal & Green

Teal Series

This series has been enjoying considerable success since the middle of the nineteenth century. They were used mainly in the lakes of Scotland, and W. C. Stewart in his book *The Practical Angler*, published in 1857, traces all the patterns back to the early 1800s.

The body colours are red, green, yellow, claret, silver, and black—the latter being a great favourite on Loch Awe especially for early-season brown trout.

Teal & Red

Hooks: Down-eyed 10–14;
   8 for sea trout
Thread: Black
Tail: Golden Pheasant tippet
   fibres
Body: Red seal's fur
Ribbing: Fine oval silver
   tinsel
Hackle: Light-red hen
Wings: Teal flank feathers
Head: Black

1.

At the bend of the hook, tie in a few fibres of Golden Pheasant tippet feather to form the tail of the fly. At the same point, tie in a length of fine oval silver tinsel. This is the rib. Dub the red seal's fur onto the tying thread.

2.

Wind the dubbed thread down the hook shank. Follow with the rib.

3.

At the point shown, tie in a false hackle of light-red hen.

4.

Select four strips of barred teal flank feathers from a left and right feather, place them together, and tie them on top of the hook. Complete the fly with a neat head.

Teal & Green

Hooks: Down-eyed 10–14
Thread: Black
Tail: Golden Pheasant tippets
Body: Green seal's fur
Ribbing: Fine oval silver
   tinsel
Hackle: Black hen
Wings: Barred teal flank
   feathers
Head: Black

Teal Blue & Silver

I have left the Teal Blue & Silver to the last in this list, as it has earned its own place in fly-fishing history as a truly fine sea-trout fly. Unlike the rest of the series, it does not have a seal's fur body, but a flat silver tinsel one.

Hook: 8
Thread: Black
Tail: Golden Pheasant tippet
   fibres
Body: Flat silver tinsel
Ribbing: Fine oval silver
   tinsel
Hackle: Bright blue cock
Wings: Teal flank feathers
Head: Black

Waterhen Bloa

A fly that excels itself in the spring-time, when the Large Dark Olive is hatching. This pattern does tend to be overdressed. It really does not want more than three turns of hackle and the fibres should be set pointing slightly to the rear. The hackle from the Waterhen's wing can be substituted with one from the Moorhen's wing.

Hooks: Down-eyed 12–14
Thread: Black
Body: Yellow silk, sparsely dubbed with the fur from a mole or water rat
Hackle: The smoky grey undercovert feather found on the second row from the top edge of a Waterhen wing
Head: Black

1.
Tie in the yellow silk at the bend of the hook and dub it sparsely with mole's fur.

2.
Wind the dubbed silk back up the shank to form the body. Tie off.

3.
Tie in the hackle of the particular feather from the Waterhen's wing.

4.
Finish with a neat head and varnish.

Watson's Fancy

An old loch pattern and still very popular in Scotland that has caught many sea trout. It is tied in the same way as the Mallard & Claret (*page 81*).

Hooks: Down-eyed 8–12
Thread: Black
Tail: Golden Pheasant crest feather
Body: Rear half red seal's fur, front half black seal's fur
Ribbing: Fine gold wire
Hackle: Black
Wings: Goose tail (dyed black)
Cheeks (optional): Jungle Cock (or substitute)
Head: Black

Wee Doubles

Very popular in Scotland on the lakes, these flies also play a very important part in sea-trout fishing. There are many favourites: the Butchers, Black Pennel, Mallard & Claret, Peter Ross, William's Favourite, to name but a few. They are usually tied on down-eyed 12–16 hooks.

The tying is exactly the same as for the single hook.

In the photograph, the upper wee double is a Bloody Butcher and the lower is a Black Pennell.

Wickham's Fancy

A representative selection of traditional wet flies would not be complete without this pattern. There are many conflicting reports as to its origin. It originated without doubt in Winchester in England. In the 1880s, a Captain John Wickham supposedly asked G. Currell, a professional fly-dresser, to tie some Wickham's Fancys for him, copying to a supplied pattern. Later in 1905, a Doctor T. C. Wickham asked his local flytier to tie some for him, and he gave from memory the dressing of a fly that had caught fish for a friend one afternoon when all else had failed. Most schools of thought tend to think that the doctor's dressing was probably the one from which today's pattern is derived.

It does not represent any particular natural but it has been very successful from the waters of the American West through Europe to New Zealand, catching fish in all sorts of waters, at any level and fished wet or dry. The step-by-step description is in the dry-fly section, page 63.

The wet version is tied using the same materials, but the wing is tied in last, not first as in the dry pattern. As with most wet flies, the wing slopes backward over the body.

Hooks: Down-eyed 12–16
Thread: Yellow or black, if preferred
Tail: Red cock-hackle fibres
Body: Flat gold tinsel, hackled palmer-fashion with red cock
Ribbing: Fine gold wire
Wings: Starling
Head: Yellow or black

Williams' Favourite

A highly successful pattern of Welsh origin and attributed to the father of A. Courtney Williams, the author of *A Dictionary of Trout Flies*.

It is an easy spider pattern to tie and is very often found in Wales and Scotland tied on wee-double hooks and is very popular for sea trout. Its popular cousin, the Black Pennell, differs only in the tail as it has Golden Pheasant tippets instead of black cock-hackle fibres.

Hooks: Down-eyed 8–14
Thread: Black
Tail: Black cock-hackle fibres
Body: Black silk
Ribbing: Oval silver tinsel
Hackle: Black cock (some prefer hen)
Head: Black

1.
Take the thread down to the bend of the hook and tie in the tail. At the same point, tie in a length of oval silver tinsel. Return the thread up the shank and tie in a length of black floss.

2.
Form the body by winding the floss down and back along the hook shank; follow this with the ribbing and cut off the surplus.

3.
Wind on a black hackle and complete the fly with a whip finish and varnish.

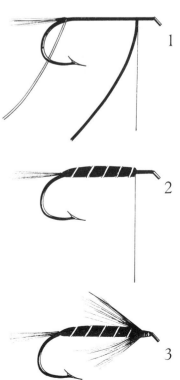

Woodcock & Claret

Woodcock Series

Another traditional series of patterns from Scotland. On the Scottish lakes the Woodcock & Mixed is still very popular. Other variants are red, green, claret, yellow, and hare's ear. The photograph shows Woodcock & Claret. The pattern is tied in the same way as the Mallard & Claret, and the step-by-step numbers refer to the drawings on page 81.

Hooks: Down-eyed 10–14
Thread: To match the body colour
Tail: Golden Pheasant tippet feather
Body: Seal's fur
Ribbing: Silver tinsel
Hackle: Natural dark-red game. Some Scottish flytiers prefer black

Wings: Slip from a left and right wing quill of woodcock
Head: Black

1.
At the bend, tie in a few fibres of Golden Pheasant tippet feather to form the tail. At the same point, tie in a length of oval silver tinsel. Dub the yellow seal's fur onto the tying thread.

2.
Wind down the hook shank to form the body. Follow with the ribbing.

3.
At the point shown, tie in a false hackle of natural dark-red game.

4.
Select two strips of woodcock wing quill from a left and right feather, place them together, and tie them on top of the hook. Finish the head off with varnish.

Zulu

A fly that has had much success over the years. It is a variation of the old palmered fly and the dressing can be traced back to the seventeenth century, although I have been unable to trace anyone responsible for it.

It is an imitation of various kinds of beetle. It can be fished wet or dry.

It has a variant, the Blue Zulu, where the black hackle is substituted by a blue. I have often been asked by anglers for the body to have black ostrich herl instead of wool. This was, in fact, a popular modification earlier in the century.

The Zulu is tied in the same way as the Soldier Palmer and the step-by-step numbers refer to the drawings on page 87.

Hooks: Down-eyed 10–14
Thread: Black
Tail: Scarlet/red wool
Body: Black seal's fur, black wool, or black ostrich herl
Rib: Flat silver tinsel
Hackle: Black cock
Head: Black

1.
At the bend of the hook, tie in a length of flat silver tinsel. At that point, tie in the red wool.

2.
Wind the wool up the shank to make the body. Tie in the black cock hackle.

3.
Palmer the black hackle down the body and secure with the ribbing tinsel. Take the tinsel down the shank.

4.
Cut off surplus and remove hackle point at the rear. Varnish the head in the usual way.

This lovely stretch of water is now a reserve for migratory birds. This photograph was taken a few years ago, and the two brace of trout were caught by the author fishing with a size 14 Soldier Palmer.

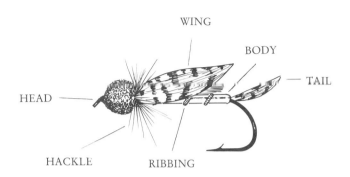

This section covers the long-shanked attractor flies which, paradoxically enough, are not considered to imitate any flies at all. Most fishermen believe that they imitate the small baitfish that are found in practically every kind of water, be it river, stream, lake, or reservoir. Despite this, they bear no resemblance to any specific baitfish, being very often brightly coloured. Many believe that they whet the fish's curiosity more than its appetite, but whatever they do, they certainly attract the fish.

Ninety-five per cent of all lures and streamers are fished below the surface of the water, so the choice of fishing line is highly important. This has led to a vast array of line types and colours: fast sink, slow sink, high density, tip sink, and so on. These lines bring the fly down to the right depth and "set it up" correctly for the prowling fish. Many fishermen fish the fly jerkily, by stripping it in short, sharp jerks. Some flies, such as the Muddler Minnow and some of the Hoppers, are fished skittering across the surface of the water.

In the United States, the term "streamer" is used for feather-winged patterns, while hair-winged patterns are called "bucktails". The originator of the streamer is said to be Herbert L. Welch of the magnificently named Mooselookmeguntic in Maine, who claimed that he tied the first streamer in 1901. Since then, streamers have increased in popularity and are now used for all kinds of game fish, not only for salmon and trout.

In Great Britain, where the term "lure" is used (and that is just what the fly does—it lures the fish!), the famous Jersey Herd was devised by T.C. Ivens in the 1950s, and this type of fly has killed fish all over the world, being the model for many of today's attractor patterns. These flies are especially popular in reservoirs and put-and-take ponds and lakes all over the world.

Ace of Spades

This pattern arrived in the early 1970s and was the brainchild of David Collyer. He tied the wing in the Matuka style (which originated in New Zealand) and what we had was another variation of the Black Lure. Its success was immediate and it has to some effect replaced the Black Lure in the reservoir fly boxes. It can be fished at all levels.

A cousin of the Red Queen *(page 114)*, it is tied in the same way.

Hooks: Down-eyed 6 –10 long shank
Thread: Black
Body: Black chenille
Ribbing: Oval silver tinsel
Wing: Black hen hackle tied as a crest (sometimes known as an overwing)
Overwing: Dark bronze mallard
Hackle: Guinea Fowl
Head: Black

Alexandra

This fly, illustrated above, is tied in the same way as the wet fly *(page 68)*.

Hooks: Down-eyed 6 –10 long shank
Thread: Black
Tail: Scarlet ibis or substitute such as goose or duck
Body: Flat silver tinsel
Hackle: Black cock
Wing: Peacock sword herl and scarlet ibis or substitute
Head: Black

Ace of Spades

Appetiser

First created in 1973 by Bob Church specifically for the bigger shoal-chasing trout in the latter part of the season. It has proved to be very successful and is an excellent all-round still-water lure. As a matter of interest, a 14-pound (5.5 kg) sea-liced salmon was landed on one of the lower Tay beats with this pattern in the late spring of 1984.

Hooks: Down-eyed 6–10
long shank
Thread: Black (or white, if a
white head is required)
Tail: Green, orange, and sil-
ver mallard fibres mixed
together
Body: White chenille
Ribbing: Silver tinsel
Wing: White marabou
Overwing: Natural grey
squirrel tail

Throat Hackle: Same as tail
Head: Black or white

1.

Take the black tying thread down to the bend of the hook and tie in a bunch of green, orange, and silver mallard fibres mixed together to form the tail. At the same place, tie in a length of silver tinsel for the ribbing and a length of white chenille which will form the body.

2.

Return the tying thread back along the shank and after it wind the white chenille tightly. Follow with the ribbing. Tie off.

3.

Select the wing of marabou herl which should be just longer than the hook. Tie off and select some natural

grey squirrel which is then tied over the marabou.

4.

Tie in the throat hackle (same mixture as the tail). Whip, varnish and finish in the usual way.

The Undertaker

Baby Doll

A pattern that has killed many fish, has many variants, and is usually tied with Dayglo (fluorescent) nylon wool or Sirdar baby wool. The all-white pattern is probably the most popular, with the white body and fluorescent lime-green backed pattern running a very close second. Originally tied by Brian Kench for the Ravensthorpe reservoir in the early 1970s.

Hooks: Down-eyed 6–10
  long shank
Thread: Black
Tail: Fluorescent wool
Body: As tail
Head: Black

1.

Tie in two strips of wool at the end of the hook and take the thread back towards the eye. There, tie in a further strip of wool, leaving enough room to form the head.

2.

Wind the single strand of wool back and forth down the hook shank to form a fish-like body. Cut off the surplus.

3.

Take the two strands of wool over the back of the fly, tie off, and trim off the excess wool. Form head of the fly. Tease out the wool to form the tail.

When tied all-black with a silver ribbing, it is called The Undertaker (*above*).

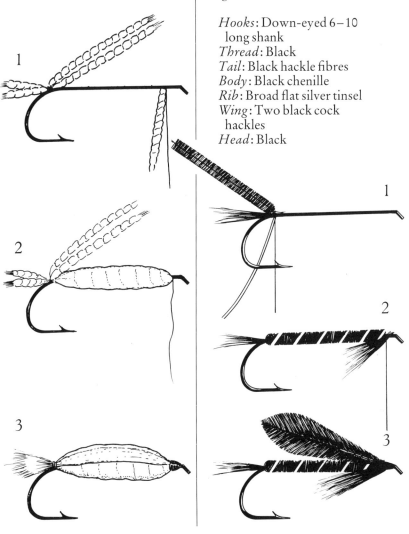

Black Chenille

There are many variants to this pattern but the original Bob Church pattern should have a cock-hackle wing.

Hooks: Down-eyed 6–10
  long shank
Thread: Black
Tail: Black hackle fibres
Body: Black chenille
Rib: Broad flat silver tinsel
Wing: Two black cock
  hackles
Head: Black

1.

At the bend of the hook, tie in a bunch of black hackle fibres, a length of black chenille, and the silver tinsel rib.

2.

Wind the chenille up the hook shank. Follow with the silver rib. Cut off the surplus chenille and tinsel, and tie in a false black hackle.

3.

On top of the hook tie in two black cock or hen hackles and finish off the fly.

Black Lure

This is one of the first lures to be tied and is considered the father of the famous Ace of Spades.

Hooks: Down-eyed 6–10 long shank
Thread: Black
Body: Black floss
Ribbing: Fine oval silver tinsel
Wings: Black cock hackle
Hackle: Black cock
Head: Black

1.

Take the tying thread down the shank to the bend of the hook and tie in a length of black floss. At the same place, tie in a length of oval silver tinsel.

Black Lure

2.

Return the thread back towards the eye, and then wind the black floss tightly along the shank. Follow with the ribbing to form the body. Tie off at the eye.

3.

Select the wings and tie in on top of the hook. Tie off.

4.

Add the throat hackle. Whip, varnish, and finish in the usual way.

Black & Orange Marabou

Another of the earliest patterns to use marabou, this was designed by Taff Price.

Hooks: Down-eyed 6–10 long shank
Thread: Black
Tail: Orange cock fibres
Body: Flat gold tinsel
Ribbing: Oval gold tinsel
Wings: Black marabou
Cheek (optional): Jungle Cock (or substitute)
Throat: Orange cock hackle
Head: Black

Black & Orange Marabou

1.

Take the thread down the hook. Tie in a length of oval gold tinsel and a bunch of orange cock-hackle fibres at the bend. Return the thread up the shank and tie in a strip of flat gold tinsel.

2.

Wind the flat gold tinsel down the shank and back. Follow with the rib, and tie in a bunch of orange cock-hackle fibres.

3.

Select a bunch of black marabou and tie in on top of the shank to form the wing. On either side, tie in a Jungle Cock or substitute feather. Finish the fly in the usual way.

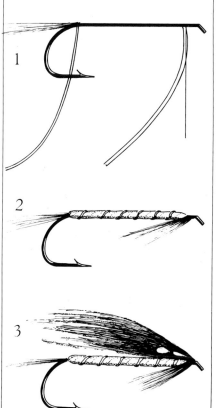

Black-nose Dace

Hooks: Down-eyed 6–10
Thread: Black
Tag: Red wool
Body: Flat silver tinsel
Rib: Silver oval tinsel
Wing: White bucktail on the
 bottom, black bucktail in the
 middle, and natural brown
 bucktail on top (the black
 bucktail should only be 2/3
 of the white and brown
 bucktail)
Cheeks (optional): Jungle
 Cock
Head: Black

1.
Take the tying thread down the hook to the bend and tie in the red wool tag. At the same place, tie in a length of oval silver tinsel. Return the thread back up the shank and tie in a length of flat silver tinsel near the eye.

2.
Make the body by winding the flat tinsel down the hook and back again. Follow with the oval tinsel ribbing.

3.
Now tie the white bucktail on top of the hook. Tie over this the black bucktail, which is about 2/3 the length of the white. Finally, tie over the brown bucktail, which is the same length as the white.

4.
Whip, varnish, and finish in the usual way.

Church Fry

This pattern was designed in 1962 by Bob Church to represent a perch fry when the Ravensthorpe became alive with them and there was no satisfactory pattern to catch fish at the time. The pattern is dressed in the same manner as the Sweeney Todd (*page 115*) only using the different materials.

Hooks: Down-eyed 6–10
   long shank
Thread: Black
Body: Orange chenille
Rib: Silver tinsel
Collar: Magenta daylight
   fluorescent floss or wool
Hackle: Crimson-dyed
   hackle fibres
Wing: Grey squirrel tail
Head: Black

Dambuster

To all intents and purposes, this is a long-shanked Red Tag and a very successful pattern on the reservoirs.

Hooks: Down-eyed 6–10
   long shank
Thread: Black
Tail: Fluorescent red wool
Body: Peacock herl
Hackle: Natural red cock
   hackles as shown in illustra-
   tion
Head: Black

1.
Take the tying thread down to the bend of the hook and tie in the fluorescent red wool tag. At the same point, tie in the peacock herl.

2.
Return the thread back along the shank to the eye. Varnish the shank.

3.
Make the peacock herl into a rope and wind thinly back up the hook over the wet varnish to make the body. Tie off.

4.
Tie in the hackles and finish in the usual way.

Whisky Dog Nobbler

Black Dog Nobbler

Dog Nobbler

The most popular pattern to hit the still-water trout-fishing industry for a long time. Tied with marabou and chenille with a weighted head. The variants are legion but white, black, or whisky patterns are probably the most popular. It is easy to tie.

Hooks: Down-eyed 6–10 long shank
Thread: Colour of body
Tail: Marabou
Body: Chenille
Hackle (optional): Same as tail
Head: Weighted and varnished; it can have a painted eye

1.
Weight the hook shank. A drop of superglue (an extremely fast-drying and hard glue, available in all tackle shops) aids the permanence of the head. Dip the head in clear, black, or coloured varnish. Paint on an eye (optional).

2.
Tie in a bunch of marabou and a strip of chenille at the bend of the hook.

3.
Take the thread back to the head. Follow with the chenille. Tie off the chenille and cut off the excess.

At this stage, the fly can be considered complete, but a hackle can be tied if so desired.

The above version of the Black Dog Nobbler has been tied with the head weighted by a couple of turns of lead wire covered with peacock herl.

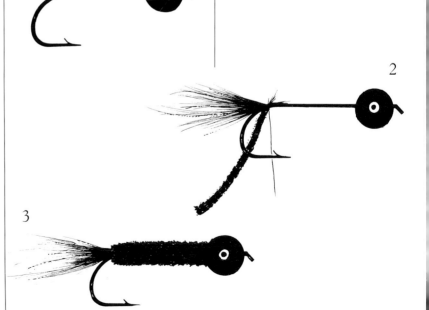

Dunkeld

Exactly the same dressing as for the wet fly *(page 73)* except that you use long-shank hooks, size 6 – 10. As with the wet fly, cheeks are optional. Sometimes, the lure has a body of flat gold tinsel only (instead of palmered, as in the wet version).

Jack Frost

Another excellent pattern from the Bob Church stable. This lure followed on from the now-famous Appetiser in 1974.

Hooks: Down-eyed 6 –10
  long shank
Thread: White
Tag: Crimson wool (crimson
  cock fibres if preferred)
Body: White flourescent
  wool covered by a 1/8″ (3 mm)
  wide strip of polythene
Hackle: Crimson cock fibres
  mixed with white cock fibres
Wing: Large spray of white
  marabou
Head: White

1.

Take the tying thread down the shank of the hook to the bend and tie in the crimson wool for the tag. Follow this with the polythene.

2.

Tie in the white flourescent wool and wind tightly up the shank to the eye. Follow with the polythene and tie in.

3.

Take the marabou spray and tie in on top of the hook, behind the eye, and make sure that the marabou will extend beyond the bend of the hook.

4.

Tie the hackle in, first the crimson cock and then the white cock. These should be tied in behind the eye but before the wing.

5.

Whip and finish off in the usual way.

103

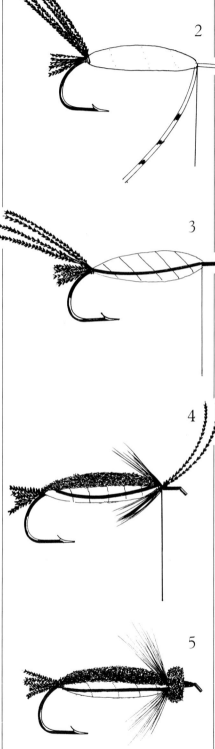

Jersey Herd

Created by Tom Ivens, one of the pioneers of modern reservoir fly fishing. The original fly used the copper-coloured foil top of a Jersey milk bottle.

> *Hooks*: Down-eyed 6 –10
> *Thread*: Black
> *Tail (back and head)*: Bronze peacock herl
> *Body*: Built with floss and covered with copper-coloured Lurex or tinsel
> *Hackle (collar)*: Hot-orange cock
> *Head*: Black

1.

Take the thread down to the bend of the hook and tie in four or five strands of bronze peacock herl so that the short ends project over the end of the hook to form the tail. At this point, tie in a length of floss or wool to form the underbody.

2.

Take the thread back up the hook and form the underbody by winding the floss or wool into a nice plump shape. Cut off the surplus wool and tie in a length of copper-coloured tinsel.

3.

Cover the underbody with even lappings of the tinsel down to the bend and back. Tie off and cut off the surplus.

4.

Form the back by taking the peacock herl over the tinsel body. Tie off and remove the surplus. At this point, wind on a hot-orange cock hackle. Tie in another two strands of peacock herl. Finish off the fly by forming a round head of peacock herl. Whip, varnish, and finish in the usual way.

5.

The finished fly. The length of the tail is a matter of taste.

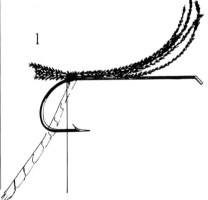

Leslie's Lure

Another New Zealand fly that, along with the Mrs. Simpson, is becoming very popular.

Hooks: Down-eyed 8–10 long shank
Thread: Black
Tail: Cock-pheasant tail fibres or brown squirrel's tail fur
Body: Normally red, but can be yellow or green
Ribbing (optional): Oval silver tinsel
Wing: Two pairs of hen-pheasant wing-front or body feathers, tied in to lie close to the body
Head: Black

1.

Take the thread down to the bend of the hook. Tie in a bunch of cock-pheasant fibres for the tail. At the same point tie in a length of red or yellow wool. If you want ribbing, tie in oval silver tinsel.

2.

Take the thread back up the shank and form the body with the wool; cut off surplus. Follow with ribbing, if used.

3.

Tie two hen-pheasant feathers onto each side of the body. Form the head and finish off.

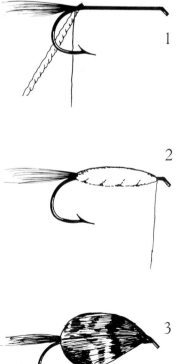

105

Matukas

All Matuka flies are dressed in the same way, the distinguishing feature being the wing tied down by means of the ribbing material.

1.

Select two matching hackles. These can be cock neck hackles, saddle hackles, hen hackles, or game-bird body feathers, depending on the particular pattern. Strip the flue from the underside of the hackles.

2.

At the bend of the hook, tie in a length of oval ribbing and a length of chenille. Wind the chenille up the hook shank and tie in. Tie the two hackles on top of the hook.

3.

Wind the ribbing carefully through the wing and tie off. Finally, add a false hackle of cock-hackle fibres.

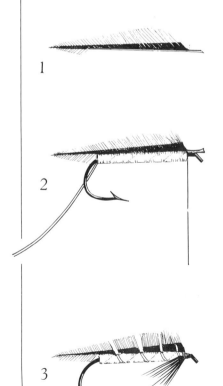

Guinea Fowl & Matuka

Badger & Silver Matuka

Badger Matuka

Hooks: Down-eyed 6–10
long shank
Thread: Black
Body: Fluorescent white
wool
Ribbing: Oval silver tinsel
Wings: Two badger cock
hackles
Hackle: White cock hackle
(orange if preferred)
Head: Black

Badger Matuka

Black Ghost (Matuka-winged)

Hooks: Down-eyed 6–10
long shank
Thread: Black
Tail: Yellow hackle fibres
Body: Black wool or floss
Ribbing: Flat silver tinsel
Hackle: Yellow hackle fibres
Wings: Four white hackles
tied down Matuka-style
Cheek (optional): Jungle
Cock
Head: Black varnish

Black & Red Matuka

Another of the very popular Matuka
series. Black with silver and black
with red have always been very good
combinations of colours for most
flies.

Hooks: Down-eyed 6–10
long shank
Thread: Black
Body: Red chenille (if you
want a slimmer-looking
lure, use floss)
Ribbing: Gold or silver
Wing: Black cock hackles
Hackle: Black cock hackle
Head: Black

Olive Matuka

Hooks: Down-eyed 6–10
 long shank
Thread: Olive
Body: Olive chenille
Ribbing: Oval gold tinsel
Wing: Four olive hen hackles
Hackle: Olive hen
Head: Olive or black

Red & Grey Matuka

This Matuka-style lure has had a surprising amount of success. It can be fished on the surface or deep, slow or fast, and is well worth trying on one of those "no-hope" days.

Hooks: Down-eyed 6–10
 long shank
Thread: Black
Body: Grey chenille
Ribbing: Oval silver tinsel
Hackle: Scarlet cock-hackle
 fibres
Wing: Hen-pheasant body
 feather
Head: Black

Mickey Finn

This is a world-famous American streamer pattern, very effective in cloudy water conditions.

Hooks: Down-eyed 6–10
 long shank
Thread: Black
Body: Flat silver Lurex or
 tinsel
Ribbing: Oval silver tinsel
Wing: Scarlet and yellow
 bucktail (mixed yellow-
 scarlet-yellow)
Head: Black

1.

Take the thread to the bend of the hook. Tie in a length of oval silver tinsel, take the thread back up the shank, and tie in a strip of flat silver Lurex or tinsel.

2.

Form the body by winding the flat tinsel down the hook and back. Follow with the silver rib.

3.

Now for the wing which is in three parts. Tie a small bunch of yellow bucktail; on top of this, tie a bunch of red bucktail, and on top of this, another bunch of yellow bucktail. Keep the wing sparse. Tie off. Form the head of the fly and finish in the usual way.

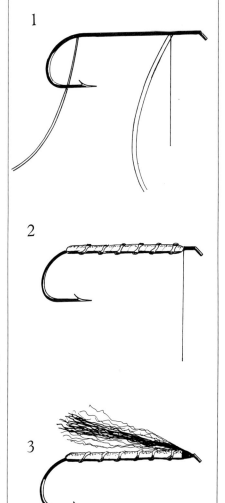

Missionary

A pattern first tied by Captain J.J. Dunn specifically for fishing the Chew and the Blagdon. A variation of the Missionary (tied with an orange hackle instead of a white one) was used by Mr. C.G. Heywood on the Tongariro River in New Zealand to catch seven fish averaging 12 pounds (5.5 kg) each—all taken during one morning's fishing. Dick Shrive made the pattern really successful and it is usually now tied with a red or orange hackle.

Hooks: Down-eyed 6–10
Thread: Black
Body: White chenille
Ribbing: Oval silver tinsel
Hackle: Orange cock
Wing: Silver mallard flank
Head: Black

1.
At the bend, tie in a length of white chenille, a length of oval silver tinsel, and a bunch of scarlet cock-hackle fibres for the tail.

2.
Wind the chenille up the shank after the tying thread. Follow this with the ribbing. Cut off surplus and tie in a beard hackle of orange cock-hackle fibres.

3.
Take a silver mallard flank feather, the appropriate size for the size of hook, and tie in on top of the hook, flat. Finish the fly in the usual way.

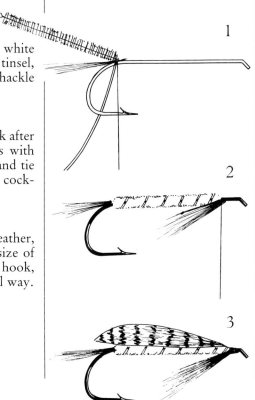

Muddler Minnow

A universally known American pattern introduced by Don Gapen of the Gapen Fly Company of Minnesota. He was trying to imitate the Cockatush minnow which frequents the Nipigon river in Northern Ontario. It became a success overnight and is now being fished in New Zealand, South Africa, Europe, and many other countries throughout the world with the same excellent results. However, it is not a pattern for the inexperienced.

Hooks: Down-eyed 6–12
  long shank
Thread: Brown
Tail: Oak turkey tail (½ the
  length of the hook shank)
Body: Flat gold tinsel with rib
Ribbing: Oval gold tinsel
Wing: Grey squirrel-tail hair
  covered by two sections of
  oak turkey-wing feathers
Head: Natural deer hair
  (spun)

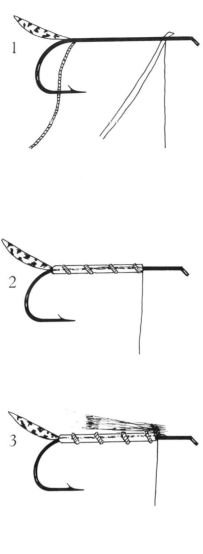

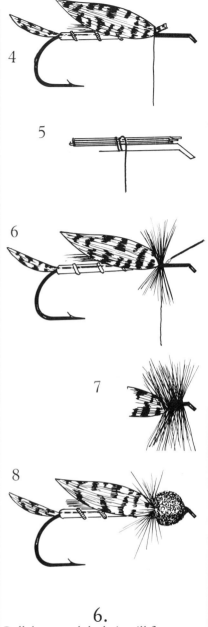

1.

Take the tying thread to the bend of the hook and tie in a slip of oak turkey-wing quill for the tail and a length of oval gold tinsel. Return the thread to the point indicated. Here, tie in a length of flat gold tinsel.

2.

Wind the flat tinsel down to the bend and back. Follow this with oval gold tinsel ribbing.

3.

Tie in a bunch of squirrel-tail fibres on top of the hook.

4.

Tie in an oak turkey-wing slip on either side of the squirrel hair.

5.

Now we come to the difficult bit, the formation of the head. Cut off a *small* bunch of deer-body hair and take three turns of thread over them.

6.

Pull down and the hair will flare out. Apply a small dab of varnish to the roots.

7.

Repeat the deer-hair spinning with small bunches of deer hair until the head area is filled up.

8.

With a sharp scissors, trim the deer hair to shape, leaving a collar of unclipped hair to form a type of hackle.

Perch Fry

One of the more successful lures using the grizzle hackles. The most important aspect of grizzle capes is to try to obtain the best available—they differ very much in quality.

> *Hooks*: Down-eyed 6–10 long shank
> *Thread*: Black
> *Tail*: Scarlet cock-hackle fibres
> *Body*: White chenille
> *Ribbing*: Oval silver tinsel
> *Throat*: As tail
> *Wing*: Two grizzle hackles
> *Head*: Black

1.

Take your tying thread down to the bend of the hook and tie in the scarlet cock-hackle fibres for the tail. At the same place, tie in a length of oval silver tinsel for the ribbing and a length of white chenille for the body.

2.

Wind the tying thread back along the shank. Now wind the white chenille tightly over the shank up to the eye to form the body. Follow with the the tinsel and tie in.

3.

Select two matching grizzle hackles and tie on top of the hook. Now tie in a bunch of scarlet cock-hackle fibres for the throat.

4.

Whip, varnish, and finish off in the usual way.

Persuader

Another of John Goddard's patterns which has proved to be a very successful pattern on all waters. It is really tied as a nymph, although I have included it in the lure section as it can be tied on a size-6 long-shanked hook and be fished at all depths. It is also one of the easier patterns to tie.

> *Hooks*: Down-eyed 6–10 long shank
> *Thread*: Orange
> *Body*: Five strands of white ostrich herl
> *Thorax*: Orange seal's fur
> *Wing-case*: Three strands of dark-brown dyed turkey herl from tail feathers
> *Ribbing*: Round silver tinsel
> *Head*: Orange or black

1.

At the bend, tie in a few strands of white ostrich herl and a length of silver tinsel.

2.

Return the thread two-thirds up the shank and follow it with the ostrich-herl body. Rib evenly with the tinsel. Tie in a length of turkey-herl fibres for the wing-case. Dub some orange seal's fur onto the tying thread.

3.

Form the thorax with the orange seal's fur. Take the wing-case over the back, tie off, and cut away the surplus. Finish off the fly in the usual way.

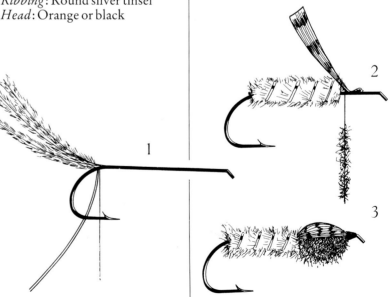

Polystickle

Dick Walker first tied this pattern in 1966 and through the *Trout and Salmon* magazine introduced it to the growing number of still-water fishermen. It was tied to represent the fry, stickleback, and minnows present in larger reservoirs. There are many variants: black raffene with red cock hackle, brown raffene with orange hackle, green raffene with yellow hackle, or whatever you wish. A red throat can be added to the fly by winding on some crimson floss before winding on the polythene. This is optional.

Tie this fly on a silvered nickel or stainless-steel hook, as this gives a silvery effect to the finished fly.

Hooks: Down-eyed 6–10 long shank (stainless steel or silvered nickel)
Thread: Black
Body: Black silk 2/3 of distance to the eye, where a length of crimson floss silk is wound in up to the eye. Covered and built with polythene.
Throat Hackle: Hot-orange dyed cock hackle
Back and Tail: Brown raffene (or variant)
Head: Black

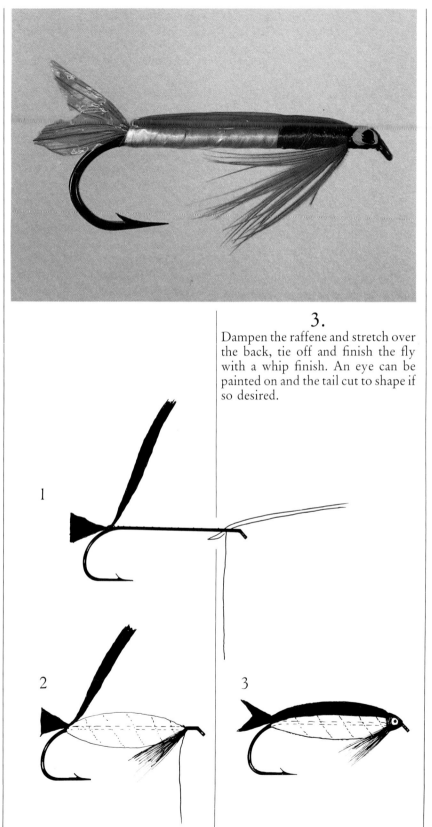

1.

At the bend of the fly, tie in a strip of raffene and take the thread back to the eye. Tie in a long strip of polythene of medium thickness.

2.

Wind the polythene up and down the hook shank until a fish-like body is formed. Practice will allow you to gauge the right amount of tension to apply to the polythene. Tie in a few fibres of cock hackle beneath the hook.

3.

Dampen the raffene and stretch over the back, tie off and finish the fly with a whip finish. An eye can be painted on and the tail cut to shape if so desired.

same time with the scarlet fluorescent floss up to the eye. Tie in.

4.

Use the scarlet floss to make a collar in front of the wing.

5.

Tie in the bronze Mallard as an over-wing. Add your white cock hackle (as a throat) and finish off as usual.

Silver Darter

Red Queen

A David Collyer pattern which is a cousin of the Ace of Spades and tied in exactly the same way. It tends to fish more successfuly on a floating line in the upper parts of a reservoir or lake.

Hooks: Down-eyed 6–10 long shank
Thread: Black or scarlet
Body: Bronze peacock herl
Ribbing: Scarlet fluorescent floss
Hackle: White cock
Wing: Two scarlet cock hackles
Collar: As ribbing
Overwing: Bronze mallard
Head: Black or scarlet

1.

Take the scarlet or black tying thread down the hook to the bend and tie in the scarlet fluorescent floss ribbing and the peacock herl.

2.

Take the tying thread back up the shank to just before the eye and varnish the shank. Twist the peacock herl into a rope and wind up the shank over the wet varnish to form the body. Tie in.

3.

Now select two matching scarlet cock hackles and tie in at the eye by the butts. From the other end carefully separate the hackle wing fibres, tie down to the body, and rib at the

Silver Darter

One of America's best-known fly-dressers, the late Lew Oatman, first tied this pattern. It is a streamer fly designed to imitate small fish and with its cousin, the Golden Darter, has been responsible for killing many good fish in reservoirs and ponds.

Hooks: Down-eyed 6–10 long shank
Thread: Black
Tail: Silver pheasant tail
Body: White floss silk
Ribbing: Fine flat silver tinsel
Hackle: Peacock sword feather
Wings: Four badger cock hackles
Cheeks (optional): Jungle Cock or substitute
Head: Black

1.

At the bend of the hook tie in a slip of silver pheasant-wing quill. At the same point, tie in the silver tinsel.

2.

Take the thread back to the eye and tie in a length of white floss.

3.

Wind the white floss up and down the hook shank to form the body. Follow this with even turns of the ribbing tinsel. Tie both off in turn and cut away the surplus at the tie-off point. Tie in a few strands of peacock sword feather.

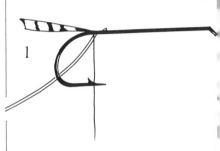

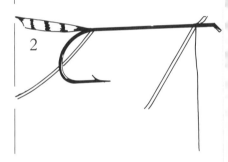

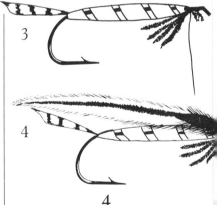

4.

Select two white-edged badger hackles and tie them on top of the hook. Complete the fly with a whip finish and varnish as usual. Jungle Cock cheeks are now optional on this fly.

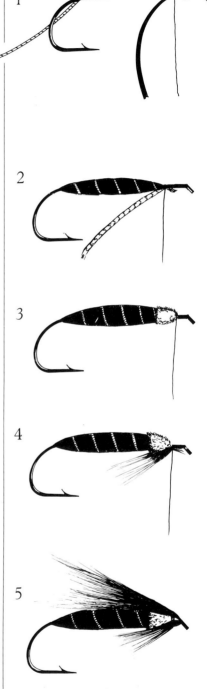

Spruce

An American streamer pattern which is used very successfully on the Western rivers. Devised by an Oregon flytier by the name of Godfrey, it is now popular all over North America and is gaining ground in Great Britain, where it is available in the larger tackle shops.

Hooks: Down-eyed 6–10 long shank
Thread: Black
Tail: Peacock sword fibres
Body: Front two-thirds peacock herl ribbed with gold, rest red floss
Wing: Badger
Hackle: Badger
Head: Black

Sweeney Todd

A pattern designed in Britain by Richard Walker and Peter Thomas in the mid-1960s, it can be fished throughout the season and retrieved at varying depths and speeds. Certainly a lure to have in your box at all times, although the hook size should be reduced as the season gets older.

Hooks: Down-eyed 6–12 long shank
Thread: Black
Body: Black silk floss
Collar: Magenta daylight fluorescent wool or floss silk
Ribbing: Fine silver wire
Throat Hackle: Crimson cock-hackle fibres
Wing: Dyed-black squirrel
Head: Black

1.
Tie in a strip of oval silver tinsel at the bend, take the thread back towards the eye, and tie in a length of black floss, leaving room for the head.

2.
Form the body by winding the floss up and down the body. Follow this with the ribbing in even turns. Cut off the surplus ribbing and floss, and tie in a length of fluorescent magenta wool or floss.

3.
Wind on a few turns of the wool. Cut off any surplus wool.

4.
Tie a false hackle of crimson cock-hackle fibres under the hook.

5.
On top of the hook tie a bunch of black squirrel fibres and then finish off in the usual way.

Yellow Marabou Muddler

Texas Rose Muddler

Tie in the same way as the Muddler Minnow (*page 111*).

> *Hooks*: Down-eyed 6 –12
>   long shank
> *Thread*: Orange
> *Body*: Orange floss silk
> *Ribbing*: Fine oval silver
>   tinsel
> *Wing*: Yellow bucktail
> *Head*: Natural deer hair

Yellow Marabou Muddler

Tie in the same way as the Muddler Minnow (*page 111*).

> *Hooks*: Down-eyed 6 –12
>   long shank
> *Thread*: White
> *Body*: Flat gold tinsel
> *Ribbing*: Fine oval gold
>   tinsel
> *Wing*: Died yellow turkey
>   over yellow bucktail
>   (an alternative addition
>   is some peacock herl
>   strands on top, as in
>   the picture)
> *Head*: Natural deer hair
>   (spun and clipped to shape)

Viva

This British pattern was first tied by Victor Furse. There have been many variations tied. Victor Furse's original pattern had squirrel tail in the centre of the wing to make it more substantial and, when tied, the wing was built up by first a bunch of black marabou, then black squirrel tail over, and then more black marabou over again.

> *Hooks*: Down-eyed 6 –10
>   long shank
> *Thread*: Black
> *Tail*: Flourescent green
> *Body*: Black chenille
> *Ribbing*: Flat silver tinsel
> *Wing*: Black marabou and
>   black squirrel mixed
> *Head*: Black

1.

Take the tying thread down to the bend of the hook and tie in a bunch of flourescent green wool. At the same place, tie in a length of flat silver tinsel for the ribbing and a length of black chenille.

2.

Return the tying thread back up the hook shank and follow with the chenille, which must be tightly wound. Follow the chenille with the ribbing and tie off just before the eye.

3.

Select the winging material which is made up by tying some black marabou on top of the hook, with black squirrel over and more marabou tied on over all.

4.

Whip, varnish, and finish in the usual way.

1

2

3

4

Walker's Killer

A South African pattern, which is found in every fly box from the Magoebaskloof down through the Eastern Transvaal to the Drakensburg and Natal. It is particularly effective when fished during and after the frog-spawning season and is often to be found fished on the point with a Taddy (a pattern that I have covered in the nymph section) on the dropper. This combination more often than not produces a take on the Taddy. It has killed many fish for me in the Midland reservoirs of Great Britain.

> *Hooks*: Down-eyed 8 –12
> *Thread*: Black
> *Tail*: Black squirrel or cock hackle
> *Body*: Red chenille
> *Wing*: Eighteen striped partridge hackles
> *Head*: Black

1.

At the bend, tie in a bunch of black squirrel or cock-hackle fibres to form the tail. Also, tie in a length of red chenille.

2.

Take the tying thread a little up the hook shank and wind the chenille to this point. Tie off but do not cut off.

3.

Now select six small striped partridge hackles and tie three on either side of the hook (you can get away with two, if you are short of them).

4.

Repeat this process three times (thread followed by chenille followed by partridge feathers). Each layer of partridge must cover up and extend past the layer preceeding it. Finish the fly by forming the head.

Whiskey

The invention of Albert Whillock in the early 1970s who used it initially at Hanningfield. It very quickly became a great success on all waters and soon it had crossed the Atlantic to Canada, where its ability to catch fish was noticed just as quickly. Now found all over the world, it has gained a reputation for catching very large fish.

It is tied in the same way as Sweeney Todd (*page 115*).

> *Hooks*: Down-eyed 6 –10 long shank
> *Thread*: Scarlet flourescent nylon floss
> *Body*: Flat gold or silver (originally dressed with Sellotape)
> *Rib and tag*: Flourescent scarlet nylon floss
> *Hackle*: Hot-orange cock hackle
> *Wing*: Hot-orange calf's tail
> *Head*: Orange

White Chenille

A less-used version of its cousin the Black Chenille, it is nevertheless a pattern that can be very successful on a bright clear day. Tie it like the Black Chenille *(page 98)*.

Hooks: Down-eyed 6–10 long shank
Thread: Black
Tail: White hackle fibre
Body: White chenille
Ribbing: Broad flat silver tinsel
Wing: Four white cock hackles
Head: Black

White Marabou

An excellent pattern when the trout are chasing fry. The photograph shows the pattern tied with a tail, which is optional.

Hooks: Down-eyed 6–10 long shank
Thread: Black
Tail (optional): White marabou
Body: White chenille
Ribbing: Round silver or gold tinsel
Wings: White marabou plumes
Head: Black varnish

1.
Take the tying thread down the hook to the bend and tie in a length of silver or gold tinsel. At the same place, tie in the white chenille. If you choose to have a tail, tie it in here.

2.
Now return the tying thread back along the shank. Wind the chenille tightly after it to the eye. Follow with the ribbing and tie in.

3.
Select your marabou and tie on top of the hook, making sure that it is just longer than the hook.

4.
Whip and finish in the usual way.

White Muddler

Tie in the same way as the Muddler Minnow *(page 111)*.

Hooks: Down-eyed 6–12 long shank
Thread: White
Body: White floss
Ribbing: Flat silver tinsel
Wing: White bucktail
Head: Albino deer hair or, if not available, deer hair dyed white

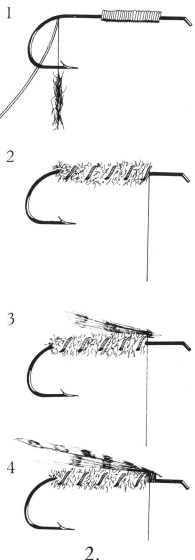

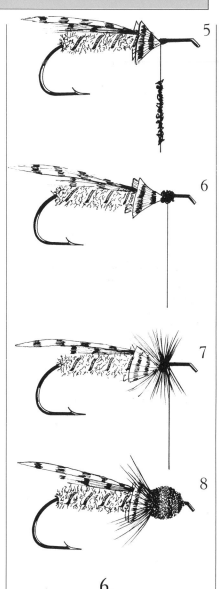

Whitlock Sculpin

The clipped deer-hair head is the trademark of all Sculpin-type lures. They are used in the United States on rivers to imitate the small indigenous bait fish found there. This pattern works exceedingly well on British reservoirs and European stocked lakes. The photograph shows a more modern version, with Matuka-style wings and no underwing.

Hooks: Down-eyed 4–10 long shank, weighted with lead wire
Thread: Brown
Tail: None
Body: Cream fur dubbing (seal's fur or substitute)
Ribbing: Oval gold tinsel
Underwing: Red fox squirrel or grey squirrel
Wing: Olive/brown Cree-hen hackle
Gills: Red wool dubbing
Pectoral Fins: Hen-pheasant body feathers
Collar: Deer body hair
Head: Bands of different-coloured deer hair, such as yellow, brown, black

1.

Take the tying thread down to the bend of the hook. Wind some lead wire around the shank. Tie in a length of oval gold tinsel for the rib. Dub the tying thread with some cream dubbing.

2.

Form the body and rib with the oval tinsel.

3.

On top of the hook tie in an under-wing of red fox squirrel or grey squirrel.

4.

On top of the squirrel under-wing tie on two Cree-hen hackles together, shiny side up.

5.

Select two hen-pheasant body feathers and tie them in, flanking the hook shank. These represent the pectoral fins.

6.

Dub the thread with some red wool fibres and wind around the roots of the wing to represent the gills of the fly.

7.

Now comes the formation of the head in the deer-hair Muddler Minnow style (*page 111*). The pattern calls for first a yellowish spinning of deer hair followed by brown or black.

8.

Clip off the deer hair, leaving a collar of unclipped deer-hair fibres to act as a hackle.

Wooly Worm

The Wooly Worm is an increasingly popular fly all over the world. It comes in a wide variety of colour combinations, such as black chenille and black hackle, black chenille and grizzle hackle, red chenille and grizzle hackle, green chenille and grizzle hackle, yellow chenille and grizzle hackle.

Hooks: Down-eyed 6–10
Thread: Black
Tail: Red cock-hackle fibres
Body: Chenille
Hackle: Grizzle, palmered and sloping toward the eye
Head: Black

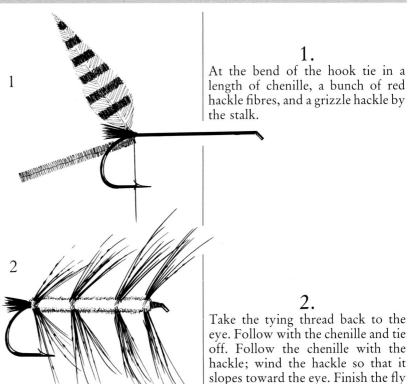

1.
At the bend of the hook tie in a length of chenille, a bunch of red hackle fibres, and a grizzle hackle by the stalk.

2.
Take the tying thread back to the eye. Follow with the chenille and tie off. Follow the chenille with the hackle; wind the hackle so that it slopes toward the eye. Finish the fly in the usual way.

Worm-fly

An excellent pattern, probably derived from the Red Tags tied by the Worcestershire anglers in the 1850s. It can be fished wet or dry and is very often used as a bob-fly in loch-style fishing. Some tie this pattern with the scarlet wool tag on both hooks and some with the tag on the rear fly only.

Hooks: Down-eyed 6–12
  short shank
Thread: Black
Tag: Scarlet wool
Body: Peacock herl
Hackle: Dark red cock
Head: Black

1.

Take the thread down to the bend of the hook. Take a length of nylon line (medium breaking strain) and tie it on top of the hook. Bend the nylon back over and take the thread down the shank, over the bent-over nylon. Half-hitch and varnish.

2.

Take the thread back down the shank over the bent-over nylon. Half-hitch and varnish.

3.

Take the hook out of the vice and replace it by the next hook. Tie on the nylon as before, but this time, bend the nylon back over from the eye end of the hook. Whip and varnish. The tandem hooks are ready to receive the dressing.

4.

Take the tying thread down to the bend and tie in the scarlet wool tag. At the same point, tie in the peacock herl and wind down toward the eye. Just before the eye, tie off.

5.

Select the hackle and tie in. Finish the fly in the usual way.

Tags can be tied on both hooks or on just the rear one.

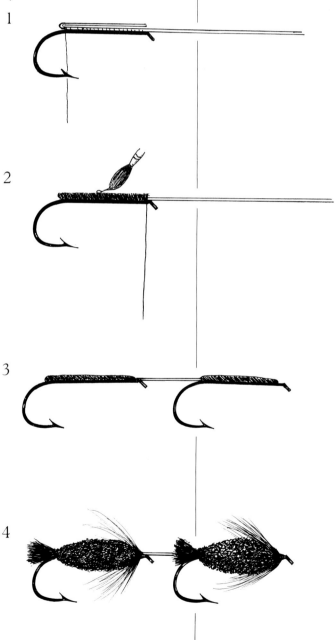

Four magnificent trout caught at the Chew Valley Lake by the author. The top fish, a rainbow, weighed in at 4 lb 4 oz six hours after capture, while the bottom fish—the only brown caught that day—weighed 2 lb 9 oz. Note the full and perfect tails and fins—something seldom seen at many put-and-take fisheries today.

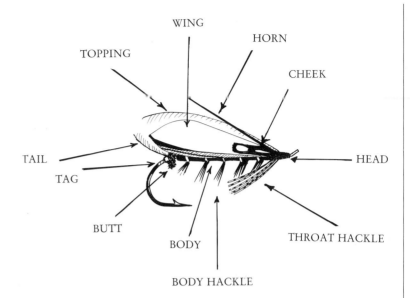

The salmon fly today, as far as most fishermen are concerned, is a hairwing, which, as the name indicates, uses animal hair as wing material. The main reason for this is that many of the bird species that supplied the wing feathers are now on the endangered list and therefore are protected species. Another reason is that many of the fully dressed patterns are extremely difficult to tie. Very few professional fly dressers are asked for fully dressed patterns today. Nevertheless, as many hairwing patterns derive from original fully dressed patterns, we have included some fully dressed flies for the reader's reference and interest.

Should the reader want to learn more about fully dressed salmon flies, he is recommended to acquire a copy of the recently reprinted classic, *How to Dress Salmon Flies*, by Thomas Pryce-Tannantt. In this excellent book, he will see the importance the author places on the method of tying, which is just as central to the making of a good fully dressed fly as are the materials.

One of the problems of describing hairwing patterns is that there is little standardization at the moment. Each flytier (professional or amateur) ties a fly and mixes the colours as he or she interprets them.

The wings of these hairwing flies can be of a single colour. Some patterns, e.g. Munro's Killer, have a two-colour wing in separate colours. Some patterns call for a multicoloured wing where the fibres are mixed before applying to the hook.

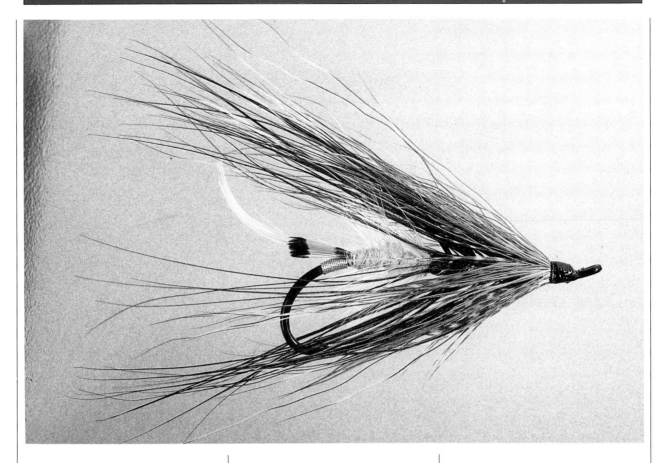

Akroyd (hairwing)

One of the best-known patterns from the Aberdeenshire Dee, the Akroyd dates back to the 1880s. It was first tied by Charles Akroyd of Brora and fast became a very popular fly in American and Canadian rivers. It has traditionally been tied on the larger hooks. It must be emphasized that the overall impression this fly should give is that it is sparsely dressed and very slim. There are many variations of this pattern. Given here is the Jimmy Robinson dressing. The fly is tied in the same way as Roger's Fancy (*page 143*).

Light Akroyd (hairwing)

This differs from the Akroyd only in that it has a white bucktail wing.

Thread: Black
Tag: Oval gold tinsel
Tail: Golden Pheasant topping over Golden Pheasant tippets
Body: Rear half: yellow seal's fur; front half: black floss
Ribbing: Oval gold tinsel over the yellow seal's fur and oval silver tinsel over the black floss
Hackle: Yellow over the yellow seal's fur (palmered); black dyed heron over the black floss (palmered); teal on the shoulder
Wing: Dark brown bucktail, over all and under all
Head: Black

Akroyd (fully dressed)

The fully dressed version of the Akroyd is given here. This is Miss Megan Boyd's dressing.

Thread: Black
Tag: Oval gold tinsel
Tail: Topping and Golden Pheasant tippets in strands
Body: Rear half: yellow seal's fur; front half: black silk floss
Ribs: Oval gold tinsel over the yellow fur, oval silver over the black silk floss
Hackle: Yellow hackle over the yellow fur, black heron hackle over the black silk floss
Wings: Two *narrow* strips of cinnamon turkey, set low over the body
Cheeks: Jungle Cock, medium length, set under the hook pointing to the barb
Head: Black

Black Bomber (hairwing)

This is a Jimmy Robinson dressing and it is tied like the Munro Killer (*page 141*).

Thread: Black
Tag: Silver tinsel and lemon yellow floss
Tail: Golden Pheasant topping
Body: Black wool
Ribbing: Oval silver tinsel
Hackle: Black cock at throat
Wing: Black bucktail or squirrel
Head: Black

Black Doctor (hairwing)

Tie the pattern just like the Roger's Fancy (*page 143*).

Thread: Black
Tag: Oval silver tinsel and yellow floss
Tail: Golden Pheasant topping and blue hen
Butt: Red

Body: Black floss
Ribbing: Oval silver tinsel
Hackle: Black cock, palmered along the body, and Guinea fowl at shoulder and throat
Wing: Yellow, red and blue bucktail, mixed with brown bucktail over
Head: Black with red ring

Black Doctor (fully dressed)

Blue Charm (hairwing)

This is tied in the same way as the Munro Killer (*page 141*).

Thread: Black
Tag: Oval silver tinsel
Tail: Golden Pheasant topping
Body: Black floss silk
Ribbing: Oval silver tinsel

Hackle: Blue cock or hen
Wing: Grey squirrel tail
Head: Black

The fully dressed pattern only differs in the wing, which is as follows:
Wing: Bronze mallard with teal strip over and Golden Pheasant topping over all

Blue Charm (fully dressed)

Cosseboom (hairwing)

This is to be found in fly-boxes the world over and is probably the best-known fly to come from the North American waters. The Cosseboom Special was first tied in 1922 by John C. Cosseboom of Woonsocket, Rhode Island, for fishing Canada's famous Margaree Salmon river. Originally, it was dressed with peacock herl in the wing until it was realized that that made no difference to the killing abilities of the pattern. It is one of the earliest hairwing flies. There are many variants of this pattern; I list below the materials for the Cosseboom Special.

Thread: Black or red
Tag: Silver tinsel
Tail: Olive-green floss (cut short)
Body: Olive-green floss
Ribbing: Silver tinsel
Wing: Small bunch of grey squirrel tail extending to the end of the tail
Hackle: Lemon-yellow hackle (tied collar-style) slanted back to merge with top of wing
Head: Black

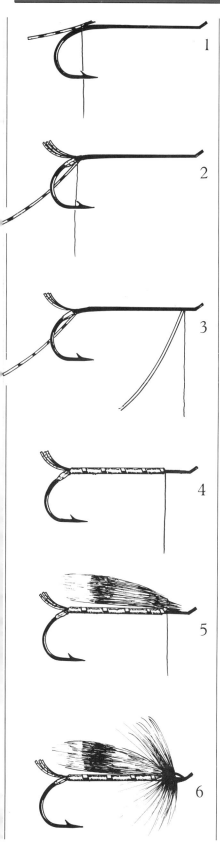

1.

Take the thread to the bend of the hook and tie in a strip of medium flat tinsel; this is to form the tag.

2.

Wrap the tinsel around the bend. Tie off, and cut off the surplus. At the same point on the bend, tie in a further strip of flat tinsel for the rib and a short tuft of olive-green silk as a tail.

3.

Take the tying thread down towards the eye and tie in a length of olive-green floss.

4.

Take the body floss down the hook length and back. Follow this with the rib. Cut off any surplus.

5.

Select a bunch of grey squirrel and tie in on top of the hook. A coating of the butt end of the hair with a thin, fast-drying adhesive secures the wing.

6.

Wind on a yellowish-green hackle and finish off the fly in the usual way.

Dunkeld (hairwing)

Tie this in the same way as Roger's Fancy (*page 143*). This is a Jimmy Robinson dressing.

Thread: Black
Tag: Gold tinsel and gold yellow floss
Tail: Golden Pheasant top-ping and orange hen
Butt: Black ostrich herl
Body: Flat gold tinsel
Ribbing: Oval gold tinsel
Hackle: Orange cock, pal-mered down the body
Shoulder hackle: Blue Guinea fowl
Wing: Brown squirrel over natural grey
Head: Black

Durham Ranger (hairwing)

One of the many fine flies from the Tweed, this was invented by James Wright, of Sprouston, Kelso, over a century ago. Born in 1829, Wright's reputation spread far and wide, and, since his death in 1902, many references to his skills have been made in books on flies and fly-fishing. Like many Tweed flies, the Durham Ranger has been successful on rivers all over the world. It can only be described as gaudy, but both angler and fish like it, and many fine salmon catches are proof of its efficiency. This is tied in the same way as the Roger's Fancy (*page 143*).

Thread: Black
Tag: Oval silver tinsel and lemon-yellow floss
Tail: Golden Pheasant topping and orange hen
Butt: Black ostrich herl
Body: A quarter at a time, from the butt to the head: orange, red, claret and black seal's fur
Ribbing: Oval silver tinsel
Hackle: Scarlet dyed badger, palmered down the body, blue cock at shoulder and throat
Wing: Orange bucktail (barred)
Head: Black

Durham Ranger (fully dressed)

The fully dressed fly is referred to as a whole-feather-winged fly as against the Jock Scott which is a built-winged fly, the Thunder & Lightning which is a strip-winged fly, and the Silver Wilkinson which is a mixed-winged fly.

Thread: Black
Tag: Silver tinsel
Tail: Golden Pheasant crest and Indian Crow
Butt: Two turns of black ostrich herl
Ribs: Silver twist and flat silver tinsel
Body: A quarter at a time, lemon (or light orange) floss silk, dark orange, fiery brown (or claret), and black seal's fur
Hackle: Yellow-dyed badger hackle
Throat: Light-blue cock hackle
Wings: A pair of Jungle Cocks in centre, doubled tippets on either side, and topping over all
Cheeks: Blue kingfisher
Head: Black

Dusty Miller
(hairwing)

This is tied in the same way as the Munro Killer (*page 141*) but a tag is added. This is a Colin Wilkie dressing.

Thread: Black
Tag: Oval silver tinsel
Tail: Golden Pheasant topping
Butt: Yellow floss silk, black ostrich herl
Body: Silver Lurex two-thirds of body, orange floss one-third
Ribbing: Oval silver tinsel
Hackle: Yellow cock (or hen) with Guinea fowl over
Wing: Natural grey squirrel tail
Head: Black

Dusty Miller (fully dressed)

A classic pattern as tied by Thomas Pryce-Tannantt.

Thread: Black
Tag: Silver thread
Tip: Golden yellow silk floss
Tail: Golden Pheasant crest feather covered by Indian Crow but only half as long
Butt: Black ostrich herl
Body: Front third: orange silk floss; rear two-thirds: embossed silver tinsel
Ribbing: Oval silver tinsel (fine)
Hackle: A golden hackle palmered over the floss only
Throat: Small bunch of speckled Gallina
Wing: A pair of black white-tipped turkey tail strips (back to back). Over these but only partly covering them is a mixed sheath of married strands of teal, yellow orange and scarlet swan, bustard, florican and Golden Pheasant tail. Again over the second layer but only partly covering them are married narrow strips of pintail and barred summer duck with narrow strips of brown mallard at the top of the wing.
Topping: Golden Pheasant crest feather
Cheeks: Jungle Cock
Head: Black

Em Terror

The Em Terror is one of the very few Swedish classical patterns. It was tied with the giant sea trout of the River Em in the south-eastern part of the country in mind.

The fly is normally tied on a 5/0 hook for night fishing and is the result of the cooperation between the British sportsmen, who introduced fly fishing in the River Em, and their Swedish pupils during the 1920s and 1930s. Today, the pattern is used there and on other salmon waters throughout the world.

The Em flies are tied rather fat and bushy to give them life and movement in the often slack water where the Em trout are lying.

Thread: Red or black
Tag: Round gold tinsel
Tail: Two hot-orange hackle tips (back to back)
Body: Black wool
Ribbing: Oval gold tinsel
Hackle: Badger, palmered along the body, and blue cock tied "collar" style
Wing: Two Jungle Cock feathers
Head: Red

Fiery Brown (hairwing)

The actual originator of this pattern is unknown. Some believe it to be the pattern that Charles Cotton called the Bright Brown in his addition to Izaak Walton's *The Compleat Angler*, though there is no real proof to substantiate this. In any event, there can be little doubt that Michael Rogan of Ballyshannon in Ireland was the person responsible for the popularity of this fly. Rogan, born in 1835, was quite outstanding in the way he prepared his materials and it would need a lot more space to describe his methods for dyeing and bleaching.

This is a Jimmy Robinson dressing and it is tied like the Roger's Fancy (*page 143*).

Thread: Black
Tag: Oval gold tinsel and orange floss
Tail: Golden Pheasant topping
Body: Fiery-brown seal's fur
Ribbing: Oval gold tinsel
Hackle: Fiery brown, palmered down the body and at the shoulder
Wing: Orange-barred bucktail with brown bucktail over
Head: Black

Fiery Brown (fully dressed)

This is an easy fully dressed pattern to tie.

Hooks: Upeyed 6–12
Thread: Brown
Tag: Fine oval gold tinsel and yellow floss
Tail: Golden Pheasant tail and topping over
Ribbing: Flat gold tinsel
Body: Reddish-brown seal's fur
Wing: Bronze mallard feather
Hackle: Red cock
Head: Black

1.

Take the brown thread down the shank to the bend and tie in the Golden Pheasant tippet and the gold tinsel.

2.

Dub the thread with the reddish-brown seal's fur and wind on to form the body. Follow with the ribbing.

3.

Tie in your red cock hackle and finish off by tying in the bronze mallard wing and whipping the head and varnishing.

Garry
(hairwing)

First tied by the late John Wright, son of James Wright of Sprouston, who invented the Durham Ranger *(page 128)*. One of the town's clergymen, walking into a tackle shop with his Golden Retriever, was asked for a few hairs from the tail of his dog, to be used as a wing on some black-bodied flies that were in the process of being tied. The result is a very successful pattern that has caught many salmon. It is tied in the same way as the Munro Killer *(page 141)*. This is a Colin Wilkie dressing.

> *Tag*: Oval silver tinsel
> *Butt*: Yellow floss silk
> *Tail*: Golden Pheasant top-
>   ping
> *Body*: Black floss silk, ribbed
>   with oval silver tinsel
> *Hackle*: Blue-dyed Guinea
>   fowl or jay
> *Wing*: Dyed-red hair with
>   dyed-yellow hair over
> *Head*: Black (some areas
>   favour a red head)

General Practitioner
(hairwing)

The original dressing first tied in 1953 by Colonel Esmond Drury was complicated and so I have included a simpler dressing that has been very successful on most rivers. The photograph shows a single-hook fly which has been tied purely for photographic purposes. The pattern needs to be tied on a double or even a treble. This is a Colin Wilkie dressing and should be tied like Roger's Fancy *(page 143)*.

> *Thread*: Red
> *Butt*: Oval gold tinsel
> *Tail*: Golden Pheasant tippets
>   with Golden Pheasant red
>   breast feathers over top
> *Body*: Orange seal's fur
> *Ribbing*: Oval gold tinsel
> *Hackle*: Orange cock (or hen)
> *Wing*: Golden Pheasant red
>   breast feathers
> *Head*: Red

Goldfinch (hairwing)

Tie this fly in the same way as Roger's Fancy *(page 143)*. This is a Jimmy Robinson dressing.

Thread: Black
Tag: Oval silver tinsel and lemon-yellow floss
Tail: Golden Pheasant topping
Butt: Black ostrich
Body: Flat gold tinsel
Ribbing: Oval gold tinsel
Hackle: Claret and blue-dyed Guinea fowl at shoulder and throat
Wing: Yellow bucktail
Head: Black

Green Highlander (hairwing)

A traditional fly which has become one of the most famous all over the world. It was first tied by Mr. Grant from Speyside around the 1880s. This is a Colin Wilkie dressing and is tied like the Roger's Fancy *(page 143)*.

Thread: Black
Tag: Oval silver tinsel
Butt: Black ostrich herl
Tail: Golden Pheasant topping
Body: Rear one-third yellow floss silk, front two-thirds green floss silk
Ribbing: Oval silver tinsel
Hackle: Yellow cock (or hen)
Wing: Orange hair with green over
Head: Black

Green Highlander (fully dressed)

Thread: Black
Tag: Silver tinsel
Tip: Canary-yellow silk floss
Tail: Golden Pheasant crest feather over which are a few fibres of teal or barred summer duck half the length
Butt: Black ostrich herl
Body: Front quarter: green seal's fur; rear three-quarters: canary-yellow silk floss
Ribbing: Oval silver tinsel
Hackle: Green, palmered over the green part of body (this green is a special Green Highlander dye)
Throat: Two to three turns of canary-yellow hackle wound on as a collar and pulled down
Wing: Two Golden Pheasant tippets, back to back; veiled by married strips of yellow and green swan and grey-mottled turkey; veiled by black and white barred teal with narrow strips of bronze mallard over
Tipping: A Golden Pheasant crest feather
Cheeks: Jungle Cock
Horns (optional): Blue and yellow macaw
Head: Black

Hairy Mary
(hairwing)

First tied by John Reidpath of Inverness in the early 1960s. A very popular fly in the summer. The pattern shown in the photograph was tied in Inverness a number of years ago and it shows the option of using Golden Pheasant tippets instead of Golden Pheasant topping for the tag.

Thread: Black
Tag: Oval gold tinsel and Golden Pheasant topping
Tail: Golden Pheasant topping
Body: Black floss silk
Ribbing: Oval gold tinsel
Hackle: Blue cock or hen
Wing: Brown squirrel or bucktail
Head: Black

1.
Take your tying thread down the shank of the hook to the bend and tie in the oval gold tinsel and tippets, which will form the tag.

2.
Select a nicely curved Golden Pheasant crest and tie it in to form the tail. At the same place, tie in the oval gold tinsel for the ribbing and a length of black floss silk for the body.

3.
Now wind on the floss up towards the eye and follow with the ribbing. Tie in just before the eye.

4.
Tie in the blue cock hackle as a throat hackle.

5.
Select the brown hair for the wing and tie in on top of the hook; trim and form a neat head. Whip and varnish.

Heggeli
(hairwing)

This is a versatile pattern used by the Norwegians for all of their game fishing. It can be used to fish for trout, grayling, sea trout, or salmon. It is usually fished on small hook sizes and is considered by most fishermen there to be the best of all flies for summer salmon and greased-line fishing.

Thread: Black
Tail: Golden Pheasant tippets
Body: Flat silver tinsel
Ribbing: Round silver tinsel
Hackle: Brown cock
Wing: Brown mallard shoulder feather (doubled)
Cheeks: Jungle Cock
Head: Black

Jeannie (hairwing)

This Colin Wilkie pattern is tied like the Munro Killer (*page 141*).

Thread: Black
Tag: Oval silver tinsel
Tail: Golden Pheasant top-
   ping
Body: Rear half, yellow; front
   half, black floss
Hackle: Black cock
Wing: Brown bucktail or
   squirrel
Head: Black

Jeannie (fully dressed)

Thread: Black
Tag: Oval silver tinsel
Tail: Golden Pheasant crest
   feather

Body: Rear half, yellow floss;
   front half, black floss
Ribbing: Oval silver tinsel
Throat: Black cock

Wing: Bronze mallard
Cheeks: Jungle Cock
Head: Black

Jock Scott (hairwing)

This pattern was created by Jock Scott, who was born in 1817 at Brawsholme in Scotland. A well-known and highly talented flytier, he served Lord Scott of Kirkbank for twenty-four years. He designed this pattern in 1844. This is tied like the Roger's Fancy (*page 143*).

Thread: Black
Tag: Oval silver tinsel and lemon-yellow floss
Tail: Golden Pheasant topping and orange hen
Butt: Black ostrich
Body: Front half (bend to middle): yellow floss with two yellow hen for centre butt, one over top and one under, both lying over a yellow floss body ribbed with silver tinsel, then a black ostrich centre joint; rear half (middle to eye): black floss ribbed with oval silver tinsel
Hackle: Black cock, palmered, over rear half only; Guinea fowl at shoulder and throat
Wing: Grey squirrel with dyed bucktail (yellow, red and blue) with peacock sword over and brown bucktail over all
Head: Black

Jock Scott (hairwing)

This is a difficult fly to tie and a lot of the raw materials of the original pattern are extremely difficult to obtain. For example, the toucan body feathers have been replaced by orange hackle points. I have chosen to list, as closely as possible, the original dressing for the pattern.

Thread: Black
Tag: Round silver tinsel and light-yellow floss
Tail: Golden Pheasant crest and Indian Crow
Butt: Black-dyed ostrich herl
Body: In two equal sections: firstly, light yellow floss, ribbed with fine silver tinsel, above and below place three or more toucan feathers, according to the size of your hook, extending slightly beyond the butt, and follow this with three or more turns of black herl; on the second half, black silk with a natural black hackle down it, ribbed with silver lace and silver tinsel.
Hackle: Black cock
Throat: Gallina
Wings: A pair of white-tipped black turkey tail (the white tips below), two strips of bustard and grey mallard, with strands of Golden Pheasant tail, peacock sword feathers, red macaw and blue and yellow-dyed swan over with two strips of mallard. A topping over all.
Sides: Jungle Cock
Cheeks: Blue kingfisher
Topping: Golden Pheasant crest
Head: Black

Logie
(hairwing)

Tie this fly in the same way as the Munro Killer (*page 141*) but add a tail of Golden Pheasant topping. This is a Jimmy Robinson dressing. The Logie is a popular low-water fly.

Thread: Black
Tag: Silver tinsel
Tail: Golden Pheasant topping
Body: Claret floss
Ribbing: Oval silver tinsel
Hackle: Light-blue collar
Wing: Yellow bucktail with brown bucktail over
Head: Black

Mar Lodge
(hairwing)

Again a Jimmy Robinson dressing, tied as the Roger's Fancy (*page 143*).

Thread: Black
Tag: Oval silver tinsel
Tail: Golden Pheasant topping
Butt: Black ostrich
Body: Three equal parts: first and third flat silver tinsel, second black floss
Ribbing: Oval silver tinsel over all
Hackle: Guinea fowl (natural)

Wing (sparse): Yellow, red and blue mixed with brown over
Head: Black

Mar Lodge (fully dressed)

Tag: Round silver tinsel
Tail: Golden Pheasant topping
Butt: Black ostrich herl
Body: In three equal parts: first and third, embossed silver tinsel; second, black floss silk
Ribbing: Oval silver tinsel
Throat: Guinea fowl
Wings: Yellow or red or blue swan, strips of peacock wing, summer duck, grey mallard, mottled turkey tail. Golden Pheasant tail, topping over
Sides: Jungle Cock
Head: Black varnish

Munro Killer (hairwing)

An extremely popular fly that has found its way from the British Isles over to the United States and Canada, as well as to the salmon rivers of Europe. We give here Jimmy Younger's dressing. This fly will certainly become a classic hairwing, alongside the Hairy Mary and the Stoat's Tail.

Thread: Black
Tag: Oval gold tinsel
Body: Black floss
Ribbing: Oval gold tinsel
Hackle: Hot-orange cock hackle with dyed-blue Guinea fowl over
Wing: Dyed-yellow bucktail or squirrel, with dyed-black bucktail or squirrel over
Head: Black

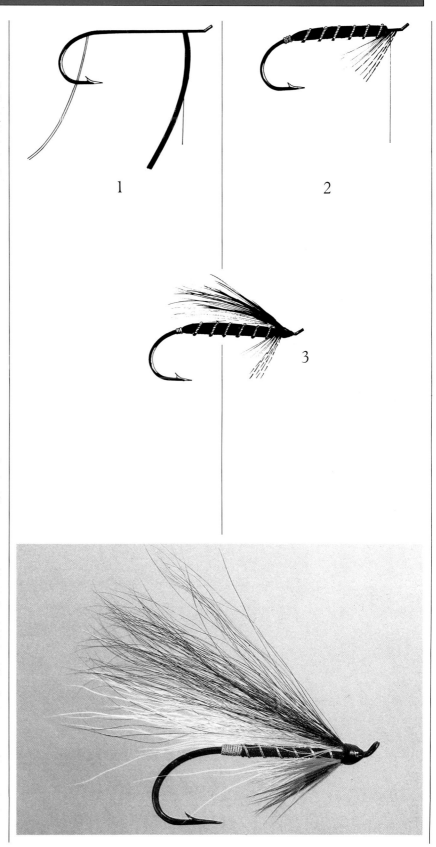

1.

Take the tying thread down to the bend of the hook and tie in a length of oval gold tinsel. Return the thread up the shank and tie in a length of black floss.

2.

Form the body by taking the floss down the shank and back. Tie off and cut off surplus. Wrap three turns of the oval gold tinsel around the hook shank to form a gold tag, then rib the body with the remaining tinsel. Tie off the tinsel and remove the surplus. Beneath the hook shank, first tie in a few fibres of orange cock hackle followed by a few fibres of blue-dyed Guinea fowl over.

3.

On top of the hook, tie on a bunch of yellow hair. On top of this, add another bunch of black hair. Finish the fly with a neat head and varnish etc.

Olsen
(hairwing)

A very popular pattern from Norway and very much in use as an all-round fly. In the smaller sizes, it is fished for trout and grayling, then graduating to sea trout, and finally as a summer salmon fly.

For trout and grayling, substitute the natural grey squirrel wing with woodcock wing quill.

The photograph shows the salmon dressing.

Thread: Black
Tail: Light-ginger cock-hackle fibres
Body: Rear half: lemon seal's fur or wool; front half: red seal's fur or wool
Ribbing: Oval gold tinsel over all
Hackle (throat): Ginger cock
Wing: Grey squirrel tail
Head: Black

Roger's Fancy
(hairwing)

This is a Jimmy Robinson dressing.

Thread: Black
Tag: Oval silver tinsel and blue floss
Tail: Red Golden Pheasant body-feather fibres
Butt: Black ostrich herl
Body: Yellow floss
Ribbing: Oval gold tinsel
Hackle: Yellow, palmered down the body; scarlet at the throat
Wing: Yellow bucktail
Head: Black

1.
Take the tying thread to the bend of the hook and tie in a length of oval silver tinsel. Wind this tinsel around the shank about four turns, tie off, and cut away the surplus.

2.
Tie in a length of blue floss and wind this around the hook, tie off, and cut away the surplus. You have now tied the tag.

3.
Tie in the tail. At the same point, tie in a strand of black ostrich herl.

4.
Wind on the ostrich herl to form the butt and tie in a yellow cock hackle by the tip and a length of oval gold tinsel for the rib. Take the thread back up the hook and tie in a length of yellow floss.

5.
Form the body of the fly by taking the floss down the hook and back again. Follow this with the hackle and then the oval gold rib. Tie off and cut away the surplus materials. At the throat, tie in a bunch of scarlet hackle fibres.

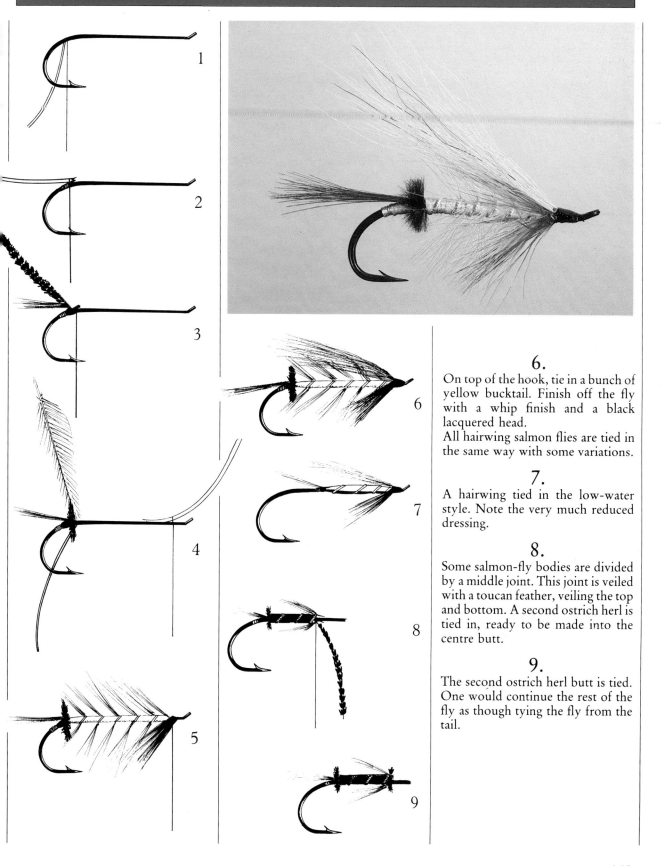

1

2

3

4

5

6

7

8

9

6.

On top of the hook, tie in a bunch of yellow bucktail. Finish off the fly with a whip finish and a black lacquered head.

All hairwing salmon flies are tied in the same way with some variations.

7.

A hairwing tied in the low-water style. Note the very much reduced dressing.

8.

Some salmon-fly bodies are divided by a middle joint. This joint is veiled with a toucan feather, veiling the top and bottom. A second ostrich herl is tied in, ready to be made into the centre butt.

9.

The second ostrich herl butt is tied. One would continue the rest of the fly as though tying the fly from the tail.

Shrimp Fly
(hairwing)

There are many variants of this pattern. It has become very popular over the last twenty years, and many of the traditional patterns have been "shrimped" in imitation.

As a pattern it tends to work far better on a long-shanked treble. It needs to get down in the water to fish properly and the seal's fur does seem to have that little bit extra over a floss body—it has more "life" and vibrates when moving through the water. This is a Taff Price dressing.

Hooks: Treble (the treble keeps the Golden Pheasant tails working well and apart)
Thread: Red (orange)
Tail: Red Golden Pheasant body feathers
Body: Orange seal's fur
Ribbing: Oval gold tinsel
Hackle: Orange bucktail
Cheeks (optional): Jungle Cock

1.

Take the thread down the hook shank and there tie a bunch of red Golden Pheasant body feathers (sometimes this is wound on as a hackle). At the same point, tie in a length of oval gold tinsel. Dub the tying thread with some orange or other coloured seal's fur depending on the pattern.

2.

Wind the fur-laden thread down the shank to form the body. Follow with the oval tinsel rib. At this point, tie in around the shank a bunch of orange bucktail or any orange hair.

3.

Tie in a pair of Jungle Cock eye feathers or substitute. Finish the fly in the usual way.

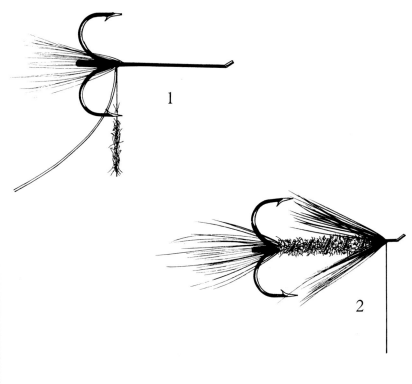

Silver Doctor (hairwing)

This hairwing pattern is by Colin Wilkie and it should be tied in the same way as the Munro Killer (*page 141*). For interest, we show also a photograph of the fully dressed version (*right*).

Thread: Red
Tag: Oval silver tinsel
Butt: Yellow then red floss silk
Tail: Golden Pheasant topping
Body: Flat silver tinsel
Ribbing: Oval silver tinsel
Hackle: Blue cock with Guinea fowl over
Wing: Red with yellow hair (dyed bucktail) over
Head: Red

Silver Doctor (fully dressed)

Silver Grey (hairwing)

Another old and well-established pattern from James Wright, the celebrated nineteenth-century fly-dresser. The version below is as documented in H. Cholmondeley-Pennell's book, *Fishing Salmon & Trout*. Again, tie as the Roger's Fancy (*page 143*).

Thread: Black
Tag: Silver tinsel and yellow floss
Tail: Golden Pheasant topping
Butt: Black ostrich
Body: Flat silver tinsel
Ribbing: Oval silver tinsel
Hackle: Badger, palmered down the body; teal at the shoulder and throat

Wing (sparse): Yellow, green, blue bucktail or squirrel with brown over
Head: Black

Silver Grey (fully dressed)

Tag: Silver twist and yellow silk
Tail: A topping and unbarred summer duck and two strands of blue macaw
Butt: Black herl
Body: Flat silver tinsel ribbed with oval silver tinsel
Hackle: From the first turn of ribs, a silver-white coch-y-bondhu
Throat: Light widgeon
Wings: Silver pheasant, bus-

tard, Golden Pheasant tail, pintail, powdered-blue macaw, Gallina, swan dyed yellow, two strips mallard above, and a topping
Sides: Jungle Cock
Horns: Blue macaw
Head: Black

Silver Wilkinson (hairwing)

This pattern was created by P. Wilkinson more than a century ago, and it has become not only one of the most popular flies on the Tweed but also a worldwide favourite. Mary Orvis Marbury mentions this fly in her book *Favourite Flies and their Histories* (1892), noting even then its popularity in North America. It is tied exactly as the Roger's Fancy (*page 143*).

Thread: Black
Tag: Silver tinsel
Tail: Golden Pheasant topping and Golden Pheasant tippet
Butt: Red wool
Body: Flat silver tinsel
Ribbing: Oval silver tinsel

Hackle: Blue and magenta cock (mixed)
Wing: White and red bucktail mixed with orange (barred) bucktail over (sparse)
Head: Black

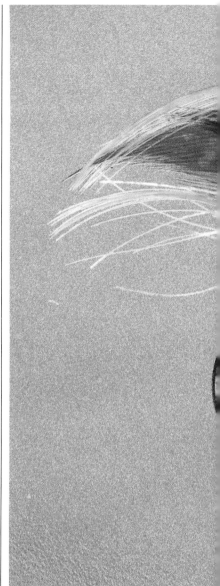

Stoat's Tail (hairwing)

There are many variants of this popular pattern but I think that the dressing given here is as popular as most. I have included one variant, the Thunder Stoat, which is more often than not tied on a treble. Tie this Colin Wilkie dressing just like the Munro Killer (*page 141*).

Tag: Four to five turns of fine oval tinsel
Tail: A Golden Pheasant topping
Body: Black silk floss
Ribbing: Fine oval silver tinsel
Throat: Small bunch of stoat's tail hairs or black cock or hen tied underneath
Wing: Small bunch of stoat's tail or black squirrel hairs
Head: Black

Thunder Stoat (hairwing)

Tie as the Munro Killer and add the Jungle Cock cheeks.

Tag: Three turns of fine oval tinsel
Body: Black silk floss
Ribbing: Oval silver tinsel
Throat: Small bunch of black cock-hackle fibres (if stoat's tail not available)
Wing: Small bunch of stoat's tail or black squirrel hairs
Cheeks: Jungle Cock
Head: Black

Thunder & Lightning (hairwing)

This is the Colin Wilkie dressing and is tied like the Munro Killer (*page 141*).

Tag: Oval gold or silver tinsel
Butt: Yellow floss silk
Tail: Golden Pheasant top-
  ping
Body: Black floss silk, ribbed
with oval gold tinsel
Hackle: Orange cock (or hen)
  with small beard of blue
  Guinea fowl over
Wing: Dark-brown hair
Head: Black

Thunder & Lightning (fully dressed)

Tag: Oval gold tinsel
Tip: Yellow floss silk
Tail: Golden Pheasant crest
  feather
Butt: Black ostrich herl
Body: Black silk floss
Ribbing: Oval gold tinsel
Hackle: Dark orange wound
  two-thirds up the shank to
  the bend
Throat: Blue jay or blue
  Guinea fowl
Wing: Brown mallard
Cheeks: Jungle Cock
Topping: Golden Pheasant
  crest feather
Head: Black

Torrish
(hairwing)

This pattern is tied in the same way as the Munro Killer (*page 141*) with the addition of a butt. The fully dressed pattern is rarely tied nowadays but is illustrated here (*right*).

Tag: Oval silver tinsel
Butt: Yellow floss silk, black ostrich herl
Tail: Golden Pheasant topping
Body: Silver lurex
Ribbing: Oval silver tinsel
Hackle: Yellow cock or hen
Wing: Yellow hair
Head: Black

Torrish (fully dressed)

Usk Grub

This extremely popular Welsh fly is a variant of the Shrimp Fly and is tied in the same way, usually on a double hook.

Thread: Red
Tag: Silver or gold oval tinsel
Tail: Golden Pheasant red breast feathers (tied around the shank)
Body: Rear half orange floss, front half black floss, separated by an orange hackle (lying over orange floss)
Ribbing: Silver or gold oval tinsel
Wing: Badger cock (tied long)
Cheeks: Jungle Cock
Head: Red

I decided not to call this a bibliography because the word might give the impression that books have been the source of all the information and knowledge on which this book has been based. Such is not the case, although I have consulted a number of books to check my references and to see what other people have written about the patterns. Most flytiers are gracious people who freely give their patterns—and even flies—to others, and that is often how a fly pattern spreads around the world, being adapted here and changed there. The patterns in this book are based on my own personal experience and on that of Taff Price, while I have received advice and help from a number of people in the United States, Scandinavia, and Great Britain.

There are, however, a number of books on flyfishing and on flies that I would like to recommend to the reader who wants to know more about this vast subject. You might want to know more about tying methods, entomology, or materials. You might want to read some of the excellent books that have been written in a more thoughtful vein about the character and behaviour of fishes. Flyfishing is a field in which a substantial literature has arisen over the past hundred years, and many of these books are a delight to read.

"The American Fly Fisher". Museum of American Fly Fishing, Manchester, Vermont.

Brooks, Charles E. *Nymph Fishing for Larger Trout*. New York: Crown, 1976.

Cholmondeley-Pennell, H. *Fishing Salmon and Trout*. London: Longmans, 1885.

Cross, Reuben R. *The Complete Fly Tier*. New York: Freshet, 1971.

Flick, Art. *New Streamside Guide*. New York: Crown, 1969.

Goddard, John. *Trout Fly Recognition*. London: Black, 1966.

— . *Trout Flies of Still Water*. London: Black, 1969.

— . *The Super Flies of Still Water*. London: Benn, 1977.

Halford, F.M. *Modern Development of the Dry Fly*. London: Routledge, 1910.

Hellekson, Terry. *Popular Fly Patterns*. Salt Lake City: Peregrine Smith, 1976.

Harris, J.R. *An Angler's Entomology*. London: Collins, 1970.

Jorgensen, Poul. *Modern Trout Flies*. Piscataway, New Jersey: Winchester Press, 1975.

Kite, Oliver. *Nymph Fishing in Practice*. London: Jenkins, 1963.

Leiser, Eric. *Fly-Tying Materials*. New York: Crown, 1973.

Marbury, Mary Orvis. *Favourite Flies and Their Histories*. Boston: Houghton Mifflin, 1892.

Marinaro, Vincent. *In the Ring of the Rise*. New York: Crown, 1976.

Price, Taff. *Stillwater Flies*. London: Black, 1979.

Proper, Datus C. *What the Trout Said*. New York: Knopf, 1982.

Pryce-Tannantt, T.E. *How to Dress Salmon Flies*. London: Black, 1977 reprint.

Sawyer, Frank. *Nymphs and the Trout*. London: Black, 1970.

Stewart, Tom. *Two Hundred Popular Flies*. London: Benn, 1979.

Stewart, W.C. *The Practical Angler*. Edinburgh: Black, 1857.

Veniard, John. *Flydresser's Guide*. London: Black, 1952.

—. *Flydressing Material*. London: Black, 1970.

—. *Fly-tying Problems*. London: Black, 1970.

Walker, C.F. *Fly-Tying as an Art*. London: Jenkins, 1957.

Walker, Richard. *Fly Dressing Innovations*. London: Benn, 1974.

Williams, A. Courtney. *A Dictionary of Trout Flies*. London: Black, 1950.

Entries in bold are fly patterns.